The Ultimate Guide to Kayak Fishing

The Ultimate Guide to Kayak Fishing

A PRACTICAL GUIDE

Joel Spring

Skyhorse Publishing

Skyhorse Publishing books may be purchased in bulk at special discounts for sales promotion, corporate gifts, fund-raising, or educational purposes. Special editions can also be created to specifications. For details, contact the Special Sales Department, Skyhorse Publishing, 307 West 36th Street, 11th Floor, New York, NY 10018 or info@ skyhorsepublishing.com.

Skyhorse® and Skyhorse Publishing® are registered trademarks of Skyhorse Publishing, Inc.®, a Delaware corporation.

Visit our website at www.skyhorsepublishing.com.

10 9 8 7 6 5 4 3

Library of Congress Cataloging-in-Publication Data is available on file.

Cover design by Tom Lau
Cover photo credit: Joy Spring

Print ISBN: 978-1-5107-1112-9
Ebook ISBN: 978-1-5107-1113-6

Printed in China

Contents

Part One

An Introduction to Kayak Fishing

The author with a nice cold-water largemouth bass.

Introduction

I needed a break.

My legs were stiff. My back was sore from a combination of slouching and paddling. My arms? Forget about it. If they had ever been in shape, that time had long since passed, and I could feel aches in places I didn't even know there were muscles—or used to be muscles, in any event. Why had I chosen such a long haul for my maiden kayak-fishing voyage? Why, indeed. It had been foolish. The wind was out of the east and surprisingly brisk for an early May morning on the Lake Ontario tributary. Dressed for a warm morning, I endured an unpleasant combination of exertion sweat and cold air. It reminded me of my early days of deer hunting when I'd climb a mountain during deer season, only to spend the rest of the morning freezing due to poor planning and the wrong clothes.

Now two miles up from the mouth of the creek where I launched, I quietly paddled the kayak to a small point at the bend in the creek and beached it on the broken shale bank. Clumsily getting my footing with little help from my cramped legs, I hop-stepped out of the kayak, knocking the paddle into the water. Thankfully it was attached to a lanyard and stopped before sinking out of sight into the greenish, cloudy water. I retrieved the paddle, clipped it into its holder, and stretched on the creek bank. Dark clouds raced overhead, and the wind whipped the creek, despite its being sheltered by steep banks on all sides.

What a miserable day.

Slipping my cell phone out of its waterproof box, I called my wife, Joy, at work. I let her know that yes, I was safe; no, I hadn't caught anything; and yes, I was having fun. That last part was a bit of a stretch. It was a bad day to fish, and having fished this tributary for the last forty years, I knew an east wind and cold temperatures also made it a bad day to kayak. But I wanted to get out and try my new fishing kayak, and here I was.

I hadn't brought any of my go-to fishing lures or my tackle bag. What I had in mind were the big pike and bowfin that frequent the tributary. However, I didn't want to be slinging heavy weaponry and landing heavy, toothy fish before familiarizing myself with the latest in a long line of fishing tactics that I've adopted over the years. Being my first fishing trip and not knowing what to expect about kayaking, much less kayak-fishing, I brought a rig that I'd been familiar with since I was seven years old: a spinning rod, bobber, hook, and a box of worms. If you can't catch something on that, you might as well go home, right? The few times I'd been able to stabilize the kayak in the stiff breeze long enough to cast, I couldn't even coax a bluegill from one of the many submerged trees. No perch. Not even an ugly bullhead from Bullhead Point. I was failing miserably, due in no small part to having no clue what I was doing. Kayak fishing seemed easy on paper. That wind, though . . . And then that long paddle was always in the way. And casting? Not only having to do it from a seated position, but with the added calculation of that very low angle? More of this was new to me than I had accounted for.

As I talked to Joy, I absentmindedly picked the ultralight rod out of its holder and checked the worm. It was still intact and reasonably lively. It's not like any fish had bitten it. Casting the bobber into the center of the creek, I watched the gentle current carry it in slow circles behind a large boulder. I slipped the rod back into the kayak's rod holder. When the conversation was over, I put the phone back in the dry-box. I settled myself back into the low kayak seat almost as gracefully as I'd exited it. Utilizing a technique you probably won't find in any instructional guide to kayaking, I pushed myself off the bank, soaking my left arm, and the kayak slid back out into the deep, green water.

Trying to make the most of the abysmal morning, I attempted to relax for a moment and take in my surroundings. Not a house to be seen. My only company had been a bald eagle that zipped past high above on the heavy breeze and a banded kingfisher that played hopscotch with me at several different points along the creek. Other than the wind, it was peaceful enough. I chided myself for my bad attitude and reached for the paddle.

It was then I realized, somewhat disconcertingly, that I was already moving. Even more jarring, the kayak was moving backward, against the slight current and *into* the wind. It took me a moment, though it seemed at the time like several minutes, to realize I was being towed. Glancing quickly over my shoulder, I saw the rod bent nearly down to the water. At that moment, the reel's drag began singing. Wrenching myself around far enough to reach the rod, I yanked it from the holder and held on for dear life as the change in balance shifted and the kayak turned completely around. I was dragged sideways for about ten yards up the creek, and, during one particular moment of fear, I slipped between two boulders that might have upended the kayak had whatever was dragging me taken a slightly different route.

I assumed from the strength of the fish that I'd either hooked a giant bowfin, known for their violent fights, or a large pike. I also assumed that, since the ultralight rig was only outfitted with six-pound test, whatever it was would be breaking off shortly. Naturally, everything I assumed was wrong.

It was just that kind of day.

When the fish finally broke the surface, it came up with such a splash that I couldn't get a positive identification, other than confirmation that it was a big fish. When it came up the second time, I recognized the mirror-chrome sides of a fresh-run steelhead. The steelhead run that I'd fished hard up until a week earlier had already ended in the upper stretches of the creek. I assumed all the fish must be back in the lake by now. Apparently not.

I waited for the line to break. It didn't. I waited for the fish to wrap my line around a root or a rock or a submerged tree. It didn't. When I finally got the fish tired enough to get to the side of the boat, I admired the large female steelhead. At that moment, I realized that I had no net and really had no clue what to do to get my first big fish into the kayak. I almost unhooked her underwater but thought I should get a photo. While the rainbow finned peacefully next to the kayak, I fumbled with one hand to get the dry-box open and retrieve my camera. Then, still holding the rod over my head to keep the line tight, I tried to set the self-timer on the camera to take multiple photos. Check. Setting the camera on the ledge in front of me, with no idea how the photo was framed, I watched the light flickering, indicating that photos were about to be taken. Just as the camera was about to begin shooting, I hoisted the tired fish over the edge of the kayak.

Then the fun began.

Apparently, my fumbling with the camera had given the hen ample opportunity to rest up. She was calm at first, and I removed the hook with the forceps I had kept on the console, in hopes of the good fishing that never materialized. Once free of the hook, the steelhead came back to life and began thrashing about the kayak. I've since heard this referred to by other kayak fishermen as a "lap dance." It's an apt term. That day, I didn't have a name for it and can only describe it as hanging on for dear life. Out of the ten frames the camera snapped, eight were comically blurry with the fish in every conceivable position but upright, and one came out reasonably well, which clearly shows me looking like I'd just been hit by a bus. The trout was never released, per se. That would imply some level of control on my part. No, she simply leapt back into the creek and swam away, with what I can only assume was a smile on her face. Once the fog lifted from my brain, I dried off my camera and began sopping the water out of the bottom of the kayak. I realized I was also smiling—a really big, silly grin. Thus began my love affair with kayak fishing. It was a trial by fish slime.

Since that day, I've learned a lot. I've learned about rigging and about fighting a big fish in a small boat. I've learned about organizing your equipment to ensure quick access to the things you will need in a hurry. I've learned about photographing your catch without ruining your camera or your fish. I've learned to enter and exit the kayak without entering the water, for the most part. I've learned some of it very well, but one of the joys of kayak fishing is that there's always more to learn. There are always new places to explore. There's always tinkering to be done. Oh yes, if you're a tinkerer, kayak fishing will keep you entertained for hours on end, at home as well as on the water.

In these pages, I'd like to share with you some of what I've learned.

The fish that started it all! The author has learned a lot since that day.

Why Kayak Fishing?

You're reading this book, so you're either already a kayak fisherman or you're thinking about entering this new and exciting world of kayak fishing. Maybe you've never tried kayak fishing.

Open water and mountain scenery from the deck of the author's kayak.

Neither had I! Maybe you've never kayaked. Neither had I—but it's easier than you think. I jumped in with both feet and never once regretted it! At this point, you might not need much convincing to make the plunge into the sport. My firm recommendation is to just try it. You *will* like it. If you do, however, need a little nudge, here are some reasons I have recommended this sport to so many people, as well as the reasons I enjoy it myself.

THE OBVIOUS ADVANTAGES

Many of us start out as bank fishermen. My earliest fishing memories are of dunking worms in a small harbor in Lake Ontario near one of the big piers and pulling in bluegills, crappies, and occasionally more exotic species like pike or trout. Simple, effective, it's the way most of us cut our teeth fishing. You can catch fish from the bank or a dock or even the shoreline of a big lake. Most of us soon discover, however, that getting out *on* the water is a more productive method of fishing. I learned this on a lake in the Adirondacks when I was ten years old and had the luxury of a small aluminum rowboat that came with my family's rental cabin. Each week, every summer, I spent more time in those old rowboats fishing than I did swimming, eating, or even sleeping. The joy of being out on the open water, peering down into the cool, clear depths to see what piscatorial secrets I might discover was one of the formative times in my life. The ability to *go where the fish are* is a magical part of the sport of fishing.

Since that time, I've used motorboats, johnboats, and canoes as fishing platforms, and my bank fishing days now consist solely of fly fishing for salmon and trout. Otherwise, I'm out in a boat. Whether it's for pike or bass, bluegills or bowfin, you can usually find me on the water rather than by the water. These days, you'll find me in my kayak. There are diehard bank fishermen, and I encounter them often. They have their gear, and their techniques, and I see them catching fish. But I think, deep down, if they tried kayak fishing, they'd never go back. And you can take that to the bank.

I could write an entire book on how easy kayak fishing is, but for today, I'm just going to share a few thoughts.

Kayak Fishing Is Easy on the Wallet

Those of you who already own boats know that there's a fair amount of cash outlay involved. There are launch fees, outrageous gas prices, and docking fees (if you can afford them), as well as upkeep and storage, equipment maintenance, and on and on and on. Ownership of a fishing boat is a burden to some, and a financial impossibility to others. I'm not even talking about the big cabin cruisers. Upkeep on even a modest fishing rig requires a considerable sum of money.

Kayak fishing offers a financially attainable way to get on the water. As with any sport, you can spend as much money as you want. If you can afford the best kayaks, you can happily lay out thousands of dollars and then equip your 'yak with the finest electronics, rods, reels, and gear that money can buy. You can go hog wild and end up with a rig that runs in the thousands of dollars when all is said and done. You'll see those guys out there fishing, from time to time, if they can take a break from the law firm long enough to get any fishing in.

I'm here to tell you the truth about money and kayak angling. You can fully outfit your fishing kayak and be on the water *for a few hundred dollars.* For what you might spend for a couple of nice fishing rods, you can be ready to go with a rig in which you won't be embarrassed to be seen. I have two fishing kayaks. One sit-on-top, and one sit-in style (more on kayak selection later). I spent an inordinate amount of time researching each purchase. I looked at the most expensive makes and models and made notes about their features. Then I looked at models half their price (or less!) that had those same features. In their online reviews, many of these kayaks

A simple sit-inside kayak (SIK), two fishing rods, and success!

A more complex sit-on-top (SOT) kayak . . . and success!

said things like "good value for this price point." That sounded very good to me. Both of my kayaks cost together a bit less than a fairly expensive one. And then there are the *really expensive* kayaks. If you have cash, you can spend a lot of it. To enjoy fishing from your kayak, you don't need to. It can be (and should be, in my opinion) a very affordable sport.

You'll never pay for gas. This is self-explanatory.

You'll never have to pay at a boat launch, though you may choose to do so for the sake of convenience from time to time. You can avoid the often long lines and aggravating nature of waiting to launch. Mostly, all you need to do is find some water and drop the kayak in and go. My biggest fish of the year, a forty-five-inch northern pike, was taken after dragging my kayak across a bike trail and down an embankment. You can fish *anywhere you can get to the water!*

All that money you save when you start kayak fishing can be put toward the gear you'll inevitably want to customize your fishing kayak. And, trust me, you will.

Kayaking Is Easy!

As I stated earlier, I'd never kayaked before I tried kayak fishing. There's no mystery to it. If you have any experience paddling a canoe, or even if you don't, you can quickly learn to kayak. As with anything, there are ways to do it better, more safely, and more efficiently (and we'll talk about that later in this book), but the basics of kayaking are rooted in common sense. Unlike touring or whitewater kayaks, fishing kayaks are designed to be stable and user-friendly. With a sharp eye on safety and preparation, there is nothing to fear about tooling about in a modern fishing kayak.

Kayak Fishing Is Easy!

You're already a fisherman, I'm guessing. You don't need me to tell you how to catch your favorite fish. All the methods you're currently using can be done in a kayak. That's right, even fly fishing. The trick in kayak fishing is scaling your gear back a bit to fit within a slightly smaller footprint than that with which you might be familiar. Maybe only three rods instead of five. Maybe only a handful of the lures and baits you're used to bringing along. But that simplicity is a part of the charm. Some anglers bring their full-sized tackle totes and five rods in their kayaks. I did at first, as well. Then I relearned the art of focus and simplicity when it came to fishing and—this is important—I started catching *more fish.* Later on in the book, we'll talk about some specific tackle and techniques that I have found lend themselves well to kayak fishing, but the truth is, you're going to figure out what works best for you. And the only way to do that is get out on the water and start trying. Like the cost of the boat, the simplicity-factor can be as great or as nonexistent as you want it to be.

The author proving that any species, even this toothy longnose gar, can be landed safely in a kayak.

THE SURPRISING ADVANTAGES

We've already talked about the obvious advantage of kayak fishing over bank fishing. What you might not know is that there is a not-so-obvious advantage that angling from a kayak has over fishing from larger boats.

That's right. There are advantages! Let's explore some of those.

Fishing Partners

Although kayak fishing might seem like a solitary sport—and it can be if that's what you desire—it can also be a social sport. If you've ever been a guest fisherman in a bass boat during a tournament or just a friendly day on the water, chances are you've been "back-boated." That is, while the boat is being positioned for the

Sharing an outing with a fishing partner can add an element of fun.

boat captain to make the easiest casts possible around docks and lily pads and other likely-looking cover, you find yourself facing *away* from the cover. Even among the best of fishing buddies, this sometimes causes frustration and friction. When a sport we love as much as fishing causes either of those, it starts to bleed some of the fun out of what should be an enjoyable day on the water.

This won't happen with kayak fishermen. Ninety-nine percent of the time, your fishing partner will be in his own boat and you'll be in yours. Whether you are fishing with one friend or five, no one is ever being slighted by boat position. Sure, there might be a little jockeying for key spots, but if *that* becomes an issue, you might need to find better friends or bigger places to fish! Fishing from your kayak enables you to have all *your* gear situated the way that you want it, and to cast to that one perfect submerged log without asking permission from the pilot. At the same time, you can share the spot with your kayak fishing friends and make a day of it. It's a sport suited for loners, but just as well adapted for a group of friends with whom you enjoying spending time on the water.

Access

Fishing kayaks' stable, specialized nature lends them to a variety of water. Search YouTube and you'll find ocean-going adventurers landing monstrous fish in their small kayaks. Similarly, my home fishing area (the Great Lakes) offers a challenge for big-water-oriented kayak fishermen. Will kayak anglers on the ocean and the big lakes outperform traditional boats? Let's be realistic. The answer is *probably not*. You can't run from one hotspot to the other at fifty or sixty miles an hour in a kayak, so, despite your fishing prowess, there is a limitation. Not that "run and gun" is the answer to every big water fishing scenario—it certainly is not—but in a kayak, you're forced to be more methodical and more of a home-body. We'll talk about how that focuses your fishing technique (and can lead to great days on the water) later in the book, but for

Angling from a kayak in a small backwater and . . .

. . . kayak angling on big water!

now, let's consider it a disadvantage in comparison to traditional fishing boats.

One of the main areas in which kayak fishing excels is *access.*

Even here, in the Great Lakes, a multitude of tributaries meander down from the farmland, snaking their way through woods and fields on their way out to the Big Lake. These tributaries offer some of the most exciting fishing in the entire country. Aside from the big runs of salmon, steelhead, and brown trout, even the smaller tributaries offer amazing fisheries for pike, both species of black bass, and a plethora of other species. In a bass boat, or deep-V hull lake boat, the access to these upper stretches is limited. Often there's not much to be had for the big-boat guys other than weed-choked propellers and the cringeworthy option of banging that expensive glass hull on a submerged log, boulder, or bridge piling. With many fishing kayaks capable of operating in *inches* of water, these concerns are reduced by a large factor, opening up opportunities that simply aren't available to anglers in the bigger boats.

And, after all, *good fishing* is why we're out there, isn't it? Often, during the salmonid runs and the peak pike and bass breeding seasons, the finest fishing water lies far above what could be considered safe navigating for an average lake boat. In some of my favorite tributaries, there's a sweet spot where the gravel runs meet slightly deeper water. By *slightly deeper* I mean just a couple of feet to six feet in depth. These holding pools, depending on rainfall, are often where the large fish fall back waiting for the next deluges of rain or snowmelt to allow them to run back on the shallow spawning runs. Fishing the seam between the spawning runs and the holding pools is where the kayak angler holds a special advantage. Many successful kayak fishermen will carry their fishing waders (or wear them) and adjust their tactics accordingly. If the fish are up on the spawning redds, they can jump out of the kayak, beach it, and wade to cast for the run-fish. If the fish have fallen back to the pools, the kayak angler has an advantage that the wading fishermen can't match in catching fish from the deep pools that are far too deep and far too hazardous for wading.

No matter your target species, it can be caught in a kayak.

Backwater creeks are also well suited to kayak fishing for all of the same reasons the tributaries are. The kayak offers the fisherman many more opportunities than the bank-stranded fishermen can enjoy, especially where steep or timber-choked banks and muddy wading limit access even further. The kayak, with

Largemouth bass are a favorite target of freshwater kayak anglers, due to the kayak's ability to access the places that big bass call home.

its maneuverability and stealth, is the perfect platform for these favorite backwater haunts.

Tributaries and creeks aside, the kayak offers other small-water fishermen a decided advantage, as well. Small ponds often

Access to otherwise hard-to-reach areas is one of the angling kayak's strong suits.

have no launch site suitable for boats. Other lakes—several in my area—are designated as "cartop launch only," with no launch ramps, just a gravel or grassy area. The deeper water of these ponds with restricted access is often overlooked and—more important—underfished. While other anglers cast for stunted bluegills near the grass-choked banks, the kayak angler has the advantage of exploring these underutilized honey holes for the larger fish that invariably call the deep holes home.

Stealth

There are some tinkerers out there with motors on their kayak. My opinion—and it's not the only one, much less the correct one—is that if you're going to start adding motors to kayaks, you might as well just get a boat. For the sake of this section, let's discuss kayaks in their basic form, which is to say when they're powered by a paddle.

Whether it's a canoe or a kayak, a paddle-powered craft offers some benefits that simply cannot be found in larger boats. The first time you slip up on a family of wood ducks or a great blue heron, you'll understand the stealthy nature of the kayak. Even the biggest, baddest kayaks cut through the water with minimal resistance. Their shallow drafts displace very little water and, by their very nature, give you the advantage of spooking fewer fish from your first approach. In this way, the kayak is *far* superior to other fishing boats, and even wading for that matter. The kayak was made for stealth.

If catching fish is our ultimate goal, it certainly doesn't hurt to be fishing from such a quiet platform. If you've ever watched any underwater video of—or observed for yourself—game fish

Angling from a kayak allows for quiet and solitude.

reacting to noise from a boat, you know that stealth is something that can't be overstated. Even with a small kayak slicing through the backwater, the careless drop of a paddle against plastic can send fish departing for less disturbed water. The kayak, in this context, starts with a great advantage compared to all other fishing boats. Stealth is one advantage of successful fishing with which no other boat or wading fisherman can compete, and, when it comes to fishing, I'll take any advantage I can get all day long.

Simplicity

I mentioned simplicity earlier. Simplicity is another of those concepts that is inherent in fishing from a kayak. Yes, you can outfit your kayak with every last gadget available to the most post-modern fisherman. With a little work, you can have electronics, lights, tackle, and enough gear to make a B.A.S.S. tournament fisherman blush with pride. But here's the thing: you don't *have* to do that in order to be an above average—if not *great*—kayak fisherman.

Though some of my earliest memories are of fishing, my first fishing passion was fly fishing. There was and is a lot of allure in carrying everything you need in a simple fishing vest. Line, line dressing, flies, leaders, camera, maybe an extra beer—you name it, and it could fit in your fishing vest. Exploring miles and miles of storied Catskill trout streams required little more than a rod, reel, a pair of waders, and that well-stocked fishing vest. For me, this was a far cry from the heavy tackle boxes and other gear that seemed to be necessary for my other youthful fishing adventures. If you couldn't carry it with you, it probably wasn't really necessary. Carrying a fly rod for bluegills or bass or steelhead trout still retains a potent kind of magic in my mind. Years later in my fishing evolution, when I discovered kayaks, I realized that the same mentality of simplicity of form translated very well into this new and exciting sport.

Releasing a large trophy steelhead from an angling kayak.

Kayaks are small. Even the biggest fishing kayaks that seem to be absolute barges by kayak standards are small compared to their "real" fishing boat counterparts. The inherent smallness of fishing kayaks requires a certain type of thinking. It requires simplicity. And that simplicity should enhance the fishing, not detract from it.

I have a monstrous tackle bag. I have a few, actually. When I first started kayak fishing, I kept trying to find ways to take everything with me. Now I realize that success can be found by selecting the best lures and baits and taking them with me. I find that my "confidence lures" (I'm sure that you pictured a couple of yours just now) get more emphasis when space is limited. My confidence bass, pike, and walleye lure is a white spinnerbait with willowleaf blades. For this reason, my very small kayak tackle box holds four or five of these simple lures at any given time. I have other favorites, too, but the spinnerbaits are always well stocked in my kayak tackle trays. If I'm out for the day on a bass boat, or other big lake boat, I will have an endless supply of other baits: crankbaits, soft baits, you name it. But on the kayak, I stick with my favorites and limit the other lures to one or two representatives of each type. One advantage to this mentality is that I'm rarely staring into a cavernous tackle tray and trying to decide what to use next. My favorites are there, and I grab one of them. And, if there's a current "hot" pattern in the area for the species that I'm after, I'll have a couple of those, too. But having *less* to choose from actually means that there's less time spent thinking and more time spent fishing. Whether fly fishing or bait-fishing

Brown trout on a kayak fly-fishing outing.

or whatever other kind of fishing floats your very small boat, I've always lived by the adage that you're not catching fish unless your line is in the water.

When I'm deer hunting, I'm always hunting, whether I'm walking into a stand or out from the stand. I've shot a lot of deer when I was hoofing along and might have otherwise been daydreaming. Like I said, when I'm hunting, I'm always hunting. The same concept applies to fishing. It might be that very last cast as you're coming into the launch that puts the fifty-inch muskie into your boat. It's Fishing 101: The more you're fishing, the more fish you will catch. And the simpler your tackle selection is, the more you will be fishing. Kayaks lend themselves well to simplicity, and simplicity lends itself well to catching fish.

In later chapters, we're going to get into things that appear to take this simplicity factor away. I'd be lying if I said that wasn't true. My first endeavor that I detailed in the introduction involved a couple of ultralight rods, a container of bait, a kayak, and a paddle. These days, my kayak fishing is usually more complex,

Even a fully outfitted kayak can be an example of simplicity.

involving fish-finding electronics, a high-tech paddle, and more gear than you can shake a cane pole at. Do I catch more fish now? Sometimes. Sometimes I don't. What I know for sure is that I don't catch a damn thing when my line isn't in the water and I'm fiddling with gear or pondering some expansive lure selection. I do know for sure that first lake-run rainbow trout didn't give a damn that I was doing everything wrong. All that mattered was that I had a line in the water. Right place, right time, and right frame of mind. Your kayak can help with that simple frame of mind. Kayak fishing can help remind you that the most important factor to fishing is to *be fishing*.

It's simple, really.

Exercise

We've become such a fitness-crazed society that I'm not going to beat this particular drum too hard, but I am going to mention it. Even a modest day paddling is excellent cardio exercise in a way to which no other boat fishing can reasonably compare. Paddling for fish in your kayak might involve a few strokes out to the middle of a pond, or it might entail miles and miles of paddling on the way to and from your fishing destination. Maybe you'll be fighting current, or wind, or both. Maybe you will be trying to keep up with that much younger friend who has a kayak that's about fifty pounds lighter than yours and a paddle that's about ten. No matter which it is, paddling is good for you. We'll soon talk about the pros and cons of expensive paddles and cheap paddles. One is a considerably harder workout than the other. But, no matter the high-tech carbon fibers from which your ridiculously expensive paddle might be constructed, or whether it's a heavy aluminum beast purchased from a discount shop for little more than a case of beer, that paddle is going to give you a workout. You are not going to get that piloting a motorized fishing boat, or sitting home watching fishing shows on the Outdoor Channel.

I'm not going to preach about exercise, but, if you take up kayak fishing, you're going to get some. And, as Martha Stewart says, that's a *good thing.*

The Disadvantage Advantage

That's right. This is a book about kayak fishing, and I'm going to tell you some disadvantages that go along with fishing from a kayak. Okay, then. What are the disadvantages to kayak angling?

Kayaking can be dangerous. It's a small boat very often sharing the waterways with big boats. There's an inherent element of danger in that fact alone. People drown kayaking and kayak fishing every year. People in kayaks are run over by larger boats. It's an ugly fact of life for those of us who take to the water chasing fish in a kayak. And, even though it happens, fishermen in traditional boats rarely find themselves in the drink. It can happen, but, with kayak fishing, it's more likely to happen. That risk is one of the biggest disadvantages of kayak fishing.

Kayaking does not allow you to cover as much water as traditional fishing boats (another simple fact of life, with a splash of common sense). Even on the biggest, fishiest lake, you're going into it knowing that your fishing area, compared to other boats, is going to be limited. If you have the fastest kayak, the best paddling technique, and the upper body strength of Thor, you simply can't compete with a V6 engine. Sorry, but you can't. Not today. Not ever.

Kayaking limits your gear selection. Yes, you may have your kayak outfitted like a high-end Ranger bass boat, but you'll never be able to carry as many rods (though I've seen some kayak fishermen try!), tackle boxes, bait boxes, buckets, and all of the other gear that a well-stocked full-sized boat can handle. You can try, but good luck paddling that kayak once it's loaded to the gills. At least to some extent, you will be limited when it comes to gear.

So, with these disadvantages in mind, why would you even bother? Why wouldn't a cheap johnboat with a ten-horse motor be the better alternative? Because those disadvantages are what the more old-school among us might call a *challenge*. And whether you're chasing birds with a dog, chasing deer with a bow, or fly-casting microscopic flies to ten-pound steelhead with a gossamer tippet, one of the tenets of true outdoorsmanship is the challenge. Sometimes, looking through the outdoor catalogs (or even my own garage for that matter), it seems with all of our crazy electronics, smartphone apps, trail cameras, and on and on and on, that maybe we've lost touch with the concept of accepting the challenge. I think, though, that deep in the heart of the outdoorsman always lies the heart of the adventurer who lives *only* for the challenge. I don't care if I catch another thirty-inch trout, or forty-inch pike. It won't change my life. I've caught a bunch of them. But when I catch those fish in a one-hundred-twenty-inch kayak . . . now you're talking!

And that challenge is what turns the physical *disadvantage* into the mental *advantage*. The challenge and the spirit of adventure is alive and well with kayak fishermen.

Kayak angling is always an adventure!

Fun

This "surprising advantage" to fishing from a kayak is not much of a surprise at all if you've ever spent twenty minutes trying to catch fish from a kayak. It's fun. The boats themselves are fun. The absence of docking fees, motor maintenance, trailering, and crowded launches give the kayak an upper hand from the moment the bow touches the water. The challenges listed above in the previous section are, for the most part, fun. For many, many years, kayak enthusiasts have known what just plain *fun* it is to paddle around some new—or old favorite—waterway in a self-propelled boat with almost unlimited capability for exploring every last hidden backwater. Combine that now with the enthusiasm most of us fishermen feel while chasing after a handful of our favorite species

Paddling quietly through beautiful scenery is all part of the kayak-angling magic.

with the rod and reel, and you have a match made in heaven. There are a lot of fishermen out there who are a bit too serious for me. Most of my friends, however, know how to have fun. If you've forgotten how to have fun, then you have no place calling yourself a fisherman, serious or otherwise.

On slow fishing days (we all have them), the kayak is a wonderful tool for sightseeing, wildlife photography, and (this is important) just plain relaxing. There's no headache-inducing thrumming of a motor and no fumes. The gas tank won't ever run empty, though your arms may tire from time to time. There will never come a time when you have to go back because the water's too shallow or the weeds are too thick. Chances are, the guy in the boat with you won't be begging to go back to the launch site before you're ready, either. That's because it's just you.

Sneaking up on a family of wood ducks or a flight of Canada geese, you'll feel that same stealthy thrill that you do cruising up on a rising trout or a feeding bass. I've been a wildlife photographer since I was old enough to walk, chew gum, and carry a camera, and I'm here to tell you that the kayak takes "close approach" to wildlife to a whole new level. It's no wonder that many kayak fisherman, late into the fall, are now hunting waterfowl and deer from their kayaks, as well. It is no mistake that, for thousands of years, watercraft not so far removed from today's kayak designs put meat on the table and fish on the drying racks. After your brief detour for some sightseeing, that half-hour break might be all it takes to hit that sweet spot when the fish start feeding again, and your success rate begins to climb. Maybe in those few down moments when the trip briefly becomes more about kayaking than kayak fishing, you'll ride the gentle current of a backwater creek. Shooting between two boulders, you'll narrowly avoid that fat water snake dangling from a low-hanging branch and zip out the other side with the same kind of delight you remember having as a twelve-year-old kid in your dad's canoe. Happens to me all the time.

Accessing quiet backwaters is an area in which angling kayaks excel . . .

. . . but they are equally effective for open water fishing.

The challenges of catching and landing fish in a small boat—especially when those fish are *big fish* in your *very small boat*—cross the boundary between the challenges we talked about earlier and the fun we're talking about now. It's fun *and* challenging. And when *challenging* ends in *success,* it's almost always fun. The fun doesn't have to come from a giant steelhead, or a big tiger muskie thrashing his way into your boat and, quite possibly, into your lap. It might come from floating silently along a honeycomb of bluegill nests in eighteen inches of water, gently dappling a wet fly and watching the small, plump fish race one another to see who can be the first to get hooked. Or maybe you're carting along a bucket full of minnows, eagerly watching your bobber and trying to catch enough perch for dinner before the sun goes down. Kayaks give you mobility, serenity, stealth, and almost everything a regular fishing boat can. No matter how big or small your target species are and no matter how serious you are about fishing, a kayak can be your vehicle to get there, even if you're just serious about having fun. Are these experiences any better, or any more fun, because you're fishing from a kayak?

Yes, without a doubt.

Becoming a Better Fisherman

That's right. I think that kayak fishing will make you a better fisherman.

As I mentioned earlier, I've been a flyfisherman for a very long time. One of the joys of living near as many bodies of water as I do is that all I need to do is grab my fly rod, my tackle bag, and my waders, and I'm ready to go. In ten minutes, I can be catching some kind of fish, somewhere, whether it's big lake run salmonids or bass in a backwater creek or pond. Because it's easy, I do a lot of it. Most of my best fly-fishing trips have been within five miles of home, on my way home from work before dark. Why? The more I do it, the more the odds are in my favor.

Sunrise and solitude.

Fishing from a regular boat requires an investment in time, even for those of us lucky enough to have fishing water close to home. The boat needs to be gassed. Oil needs to be checked. The trailer must be hooked up, the lights checked, and then it's quite possible that you're in for a fifteen- or twenty-minute wait at the nearest launch just to get into the water. Kayaking takes a lot of the aggravation away. Since evolving through this whole "kayak fishing" thing, I've actually begun trailering my latest kayak. It's not a necessity, but a choice. I like to be able to leave everything rigged and ready to go. Also, with a back that's not quite as sturdy as it was twenty years ago, I like not having to hoist the boat over my head and onto a roof rack, though I still do that from time to time. With kayak angling, however, the necessity of launches is still negated, even with a trailer. If there's no launch available, I just pull over by the water and drag or carry the kayak down to the water's edge. A couple of minutes later, I'm fishing. The whole point of this goes back to what it takes to make a fishing trip successful. Whether it's bait or spinners, crankbaits or night crawlers,

Whether it's baitcasting or fly casting, doing it from a kayak adds a new and exciting dimension to your fishing style.

the common denominator to catching more fish is having your line in the water. The less time you're messing with equipment or paying launch fees or swearing at your trailer lights, the more time you'll be fishing.

Carrying that forward: the more time you *spend* fishing, the better you're going to get at fishing. I never considered myself an expert steelhead fisherman with the fly rod, but with those short little trips nearly every day after work in March and April, I got pretty good at it. Much like playing a musical instrument, you can read all the theory (or kayak fishing websites) that you want, but what makes you better isn't reading about it—it's practice. And now, the kayak offers me that same flexibility. It gives me the opportunity to run home after work, take five minutes to load up my kayak, and spend another ten minutes to get to my favorite fishing hole. If it's easy to do, human nature dictates that you're going to do more of it. And, as mentioned previously, kayak fishing is pretty easy.

With the simplified, pared-back tackle and an easy-to-handle boat, you'll find that you won't be making excuses not to get out there and fish. Now, several years into the kayak fishing game and a couple of kayaks later, I find myself looking more and more forward to it all the time. I do a lot of it. And, like practicing the violin, if you do a lot of it, and you can't help but become a better fisherman.

A Word on the Sport

The rest of this book is going to get into the nuts and bolts of kayak angling. Before we get into boat selection, paddle selection, rigging, electronics, fishing techniques, paddling techniques, safety, and all of that other exciting stuff, just indulge me while I share a little philosophy. Don't worry, it won't hurt, and there won't be a test. I'd just like to share my observations on equipment and snobbery. I wish I didn't have to bring this up, but if you're a person of average income, with debts and bills and kids, I want you to read this part before moving into the real (and much more fun) reasons you're reading this book.

I've already mentioned comparisons to fly fishing, my first angling love. I started fly fishing when I was around thirteen years old. At the time, I had an Ideal fiberglass rod that weighed about as much as a good shotgun. It had a cheap reel, spooled with seven-weight line from a discount store. At the time, I didn't realize you needed a rod that cost hundreds of dollars. I didn't realize there were specialized lines for different species. It never occurred to me that one fisherman might look down upon another because of differences in equipment. I learned on that Ideal rod even though it was anything but ideal. It earned me my first dozen Catskill trout, many big bass, and a boatload of bluegills and rock bass and perch in numbers that I wouldn't even care to guess. I was a kid. I had no money. And, blissfully, I didn't realize that because of that cheap fly rod I was doing it all wrong. As I began to read magazines and books on the sport, I realized that, particularly in the Catskills, I was likely sharing the water with people whose fly rods and reels *far* exceeded what I'd pay for my first car. To this day, that fact causes me wonder.

Before we get back to kayaking, let me tell you about two fly-fishermen. The first is the late Walt Bailey, my best friend's grandfather. Walt lived in Westkill, New York, for the duration of his retirement and taught my best friend and me to fly fish for trout on the Schoharie Creek. Walter had a passion for fine, split-bamboo fly rods, and in retrospect, his collection must have been worth tens of thousands of dollars. When I was a kid, waving that Ideal rod around, I didn't pay much attention to what my mentor was using, and he didn't pay much attention to my rig. We fished, we learned, we enjoyed nature, and we *caught lots of fish.* I used that early Catskill trout knowledge and took it back home and applied it to our huge salmon and steelhead runs. If I told you how many steelhead I landed on that rod, you wouldn't believe me, mostly because all fishermen are liars by nature.

The second flyfisherman I'd like to mention is the late, great Art Flick. Art also lived in Westkill and was known as the "Dean of the Schoharie." His *Streamside Guide to the Naturals and Their Imitations* was groundbreaking in its day, and a classic in ours. Art was the first real writer I ever met in my life and was as humble as you might imagine a trout fishing expert should be, at home in his house crammed full with literature and fly-tying equipment.

I mention these two men who influenced me for one reason. Although I'm sure he had some fine rods in his collection (or maybe he didn't), it was widely known that Art often plied his craft on the Schoharie with a cheap fiberglass fly rod. His explanation?

Well, he wouldn't be out a lot of money if he tripped and broke it! My fishing mentor, Walt, used very fine rods—many of them custom versions, and priceless. Which of these two was the better fisherman? Which was the more expert? One was famous, while the other enjoyed his craft in relative obscurity. They were friends. And they were both excellent fishermen and experts at their craft.

Their fly rods didn't make one damn bit of difference.

My first "good" rod cost about seventy bucks. I didn't realize at the time that there were actually people on the stream who would turn their nose up at my equipment. But I met a few, and their opinions made me rethink my gear selection. At times, I was dismayed, thinking of Art Flick and his heavy old fiberglass rods, yet still, that doubt crept in. Later still, I was able to afford some better rods and I bought them, because that's what you did when sufficiently shamed into thinking fishing success was somehow tied to outrageously priced gear. Shamed is not too harsh a word, either. I didn't catch more fish with them. I caught more fish when I fished harder, and fewer fish when I wasn't taking it seriously. Now, fly fishing has become so enmeshed in equipment and name brands, I sometimes look at the magazines and wonder if any of these guys even have time to get out and fish between trips to Orvis and the ATM. I have some nice stuff now, too, but I don't turn my nose up at the guy next to me on the steelhead streams who's using the modern-day equivalent of that Ideal fly rod.

I've been "lucky" enough to enjoy several hobbies that have a persistent number of gear snobs. They're insufferable. I play guitar, and it's no different in the guitar world. There are two-hundred-dollar guitars and ten-thousand-dollar guitars. What matters? How you play, son. Same goes for shotguns and cars, handguns and archery—almost any other hobby that doesn't involve knitting needles. I'm guessing that out in your driveway there's a car or truck. It might not be a Lexus or a BMW, but it gets you to work and safely back home, maybe with a side trip to the creek for a little fishing. It works. It does the job. If you won the lottery, or got

Landing any fish in a kayak is exciting.

a big promotion, would you opt for something a little better? Yes, I'm sure. I know I would! But it isn't *needed*, and chances are the guy blasting past you in the eighty-thousand-dollar car once drove a cheaper car on his way there. All that matters is that it gets you where you're going.

In the scant few years I've been involved in kayak fishing, I've felt that familiar dismay associated with the creeping disease of snobbery. There are a few good kayak-fishing magazines and websites out there, and they contain a wealth of information. But don't get sucked in by those cover photos. I'm not going to name names (but if you've done any level of research on this subject, you already know the names). Advertisers have such influence on content these days, you'd think that there's no successful bowhunter in the world who isn't shooting a thousand-dollar Matthews; there's no flyfisherman who can catch a trophy steelhead without the latest Sage rod. And, looking at those kayak magazines, there's no WAY you're going out in the water with anything but this year's model Brand-X Super Light Magnum Fishkiller. If you can't afford one, just rig up the cane pole and go fish for bullhead in the pond out behind the barn because your presence is not requested at the kayak bass fishing tournament.

B.S., says I. No way. Not on my watch.

There are *great* kayaks out there, and the next (and probably most important) section of this book will be all about how to figure out what you need. A lot of guys on Internet forums have a lot of opinions. A lot of them also have a lot of money. When you start reading kayak reviews, you'll find a heavy preference for the high-dollar, Brand-X models. Or maybe it's Brand-H. There are reasons for this. One of those reasons is that they tend to be of very good build quality and share some traits we will discuss in the next few pages that make them pretty good for kayak fishing. But, as with guns or cars or guitars, there's also a hidden reason in some of these glowing reviews: the reviewers are trying to justify their purchases. It happens to everyone. I've done it. I have a couple of guitars that I've gigged with that were about three hundred dollars. I never wrote glowing reviews online about them. But my Gibson Les Paul, clocking in at around two thousand dollars? I'll brag about that all day long. Which guitar got the crowd dancing? Whichever one I decided to play that night.

Kayaks are no different. There's going to be a contingent of kayak fishermen out there who will roll their eyes at this next part, but those guys spend a lot more time eye rolling than fish rolling. Here goes: *You can get started in kayak fishing for a few hundred bucks.* Not just a big-box plain old cheap kayak, but an angler-model kayak. More on these later, but for now, just keep this in mind before the next chapter on kayak selection. If you have fifteen hundred bucks to spend on a new Brand-X—and you just *know* you're going to love the sport—please do it. *But* keep in mind there's other stuff you're going to need, like a paddle, PFD, and other gear, so you might as well round up a few hundred dollars above your initial purchase. Let's call it two thousand dollars, conservatively. Oh, you want a better paddle? Okay, twenty-five hundred if you get a *really good* paddle. Yes, *five hundred dollars* for a really good paddle.

Scared yet?

Carefully handling fish with spines and teeth is a must in close quarters.

Don't be. You can get into this entire sport for the cost of that really good paddle and be pretty well outfitted. While it's very true that you get what you pay for, it's also true that not everyone has thousands to spend on an angling kayak, and there are *many* more options out there that may suit you as you work your way into the wonderful world of kayak fishing. There can be big steps, and big cash layouts, but there can also be less costly, tentative steps that will get you into the sport without putting you further in debt. There's absolutely no reason the cash layout for something as fun as fishing should become a source of stress. I'm assuming a lot of people reading this book and contemplating joining in the fun actually had *low cost* in mind at one point or another in the journey that brought you to this book. And that's okay! I still think that, other than being a great way to catch fish, lower cost is a perfectly fine thing to enjoy about kayak angling. Ignore the magazine covers. Ignore them! At least for now, and especially if you can't afford that kind of rig.

Did I start in a cheap boat? It wasn't the cheapest, but it wasn't perfect, either. It's an evolution. My new one is also not a wallet killer, but it is a fish killer. There are better boats out there, but I'd rather save my money for more tackle. Do I have a five-hundred-dollar paddle? Oh hell no. I'm never going to evolve that far. Does my rig cost multiple thousands of dollars? No, not for the boat anyway—but there's a lot of gear on it, and I haven't totaled it up lately. But . . . let me check over my shoulder to see if my wife is nearby. . . . No, probably not a good time to total up all the money in rods, reels, and tackle right now. But that's not what we're talking about, right? Right. We're talking about kayaks.

Let's try to find you one!

Part Two

Gear Selection

Choices, choices. Which is the right angling kayak for you?

Selecting Your Kayak

Here we go. This is, without a doubt, the most important part of this book. Rather than make you work for it and hide it somewhere near the back, let's jump right in and start talking about which kayak you should be considering for your first paddle into the exiting new world of kayak fishing.

TYPES OF ANGLING KAYAKS

Sit-on-Top Kayaks

As mentioned in the previous chapter, the current "standard" for kayak fishing is called the sit-on-top, or SOT, as some like to call it. A sit-on-top is characterized by a plastic or composite hull, and it sports a completely open deck. Unlike sit-in kayaks (SIK), there's no cockpit under which to slide your legs and movement tends to be unrestricted, within a few common-sense limits. Most sit-on-tops are also characterized by a raised, often

The author's SOT angling kayak.

adjustable seat that raises the fisherman's sight line (and also his or her center of gravity—more on that later). Sit-on-tops typically offer the most in the way of storage for gear and places to mount rod-holders, electronics, and all of the other equipment that may or may not make your kayak angling experience complete. Another feature found in some models of sit-on-tops is the ability to stand while fishing, more closely mimicking the feeling of being on a "real" boat. We'll discuss stand-up techniques and the realities of that later.

Another feature unique to SOTs is the scupper hole. These are typically one-inch diameter holes that run from the deck down to the bottom of the boat below the waterline. While that may seem counterintuitive, the design prevents water (from waves, paddling, and/or rain) from building up on the deck of the kayak. The scupper holes can be a mixed blessing, especially in rough water or an unbalanced boat. In some instances, scupper hole plugs are used to keep water *out* of the boat. Typical off-the-shelf accoutrements of the sit-on-top kayak might be flush-mount rod holders, "Scotty" type rod holders, an anchor trolley, and bungee-type tie-downs. Of course, as will be discussed at length later in this book, outfitting the kayak specifically for your needs knows no bounds. The simple beauty of a sit-on-top is that there's virtually no limit to the amount of tweaking you can do to make it your own. For that reason alone, it's far and away the current favorite design for fishing kayaks.

But it isn't the only option.

Sit-Inside Kayaks

When you think of a kayak, you probably think of a long, narrow boat with a tiny, circular opening (the cockpit). Most angling sit-inside kayaks (SIKs) are just a slight modification of this ancient design constructed with modern materials. Rather than a small opening for the cockpit, an angling sit-inside kayak will have an exaggerated opening to allow for more movement and room to stash gear up inside the cockpit. Typical accoutrements of a standard fishing sit-inside kayak will be anywhere from two to four flush-mount rod holders, a small deck (or well) behind the seat, and a low-to-the-hull seat that may or may not be padded. Sit-inside kayaks have long been the design that put much meat and fish on the table for native people of the far north. It's of little surprise that, like most things that have been successful, SIKs haven't evolved much further than the old skin-covered kayaks used by the Inuit. That is to say, they didn't need to evolve much further because the design is time-tested.

A basic and solid SIK might be right for you.

Other Kayak Designs

We aren't going to spend much time on other kayaks. One thing you'll soon find about kayak fishing is that the sport is evolving so rapidly, it becomes very difficult to keep up with the latest developments. Right now, there are pontoon-style kayaks on the market and several types that call themselves "hybrids." Some of these represent radical differences to the current popular angling kayak designs, while others offer minor tweaks to an already established design. I looked at a hybrid the other day and couldn't begin to tell you why it was called a hybrid. It looked like a plain old SOT to me.

One other kayak design we'll briefly touch on is the traditional kayak. If you've ever spent any amount of time in a vacation area, you've probably seen the bright red and yellow and blue small, plastic kayaks that you can pick up in a discount store for not much more than a hundred bucks. Perhaps you've seen serious kayak enthusiasts with their very long touring boats crossing mountain lakes, or whitewater kayakers with their stubby, maneuverable boats shooting the rapids on a nearby river. Will any or all of these work for kayak fishing? Sure, all of them will. With the simple addition of a rod-holder here or there and a little ingenuity, any kayak can be drafted for the purposes of fishing. However, if you want to get a good feel for what kayak fishing really is, you'll find your frustration level somewhat lowered by starting out with a model that's been designed for kayak angling. Remember, the more you enjoy it, the more you'll do it. And the more you do it, the better you'll get at it. The best kayak for getting into kayak angling is an angling kayak.

COMPARING SIT-ON-TOP AND SIT-INSIDE KAYAKS

Stability

There's an interesting little skirmish going on right now between people who review and write about kayak fishing. Just recently, I've read a lot on the "overemphasis" of stability. That's right. People saying, "Come on, it's just not that important." My feeling is that when you are *first* getting into kayak fishing, you're going to read reviews and books, and one of the first things you're going to want to know is if it's stable. Particularly if you have little to no experience kayaking, there's going to be a fair amount of apprehension about whether the damn thing is likely to tip over or not! It's common sense, mixed with a healthy dose of self preservation. As people become more comfortable kayaking (and the learning curve tends to be fairly rapid) and more experienced, stability may seem like a less important concern than speed, maneuverability, wind resistance, and a host of other considerations. But there's a reason that our first comparison between SOTs and SIKs is stability: if you're new at this, you want to know.

Sit-on-tops tend to be bigger, longer, wider, and heavier boats. Common sense might tell you that these factors must contribute to overall stability. And, for the most part, they do. There are other factors, though. When I first graduated (though that's not exactly how I think of it, in retrospect) from an SIK to an SOT, for the first few minutes on the water, I thought it was the most unstable craft I'd ever been on in my entire life. Even with the three-position seat in its lowest possible position, I felt completely top-heavy in my new boat. For the first half-hour, I wished I had my SIK but persevered, knowing that "real kayak fishermen" have to use an SOT. I saw it on a magazine cover . . .

The problem wasn't actually the stability of the big, heavy boat. I wasn't about to fall out, though I certainly feared that for several apprehensive moments in the twelve-foot-deep water near the launch. The actual issue was the *perceived* stability. In an SIK, your center of gravity is much lower, with your hindquarters at or below the waterline. Most SIK seats are either an inch or two above the bottom of the boat, or right on the bottom of the boat. In an SOT, the bottom of your seat is well above the deck, and your center of gravity is far, far above that. If you're used to an SIK, or at least familiar with the feeling, you will probably feel like I did for my first few minutes. But, as with anything, once you become accustomed to the higher center-of-gravity, you'll realize it's not actually tippy; it's just different. And, with the wide berth and heavy nature of an SOT, you'll soon learn that, though it's not impossible to "turtle," as the experts call it, you have to work fairly hard to tip it over. Most have "secondary stability" built into their design. That is to say, you can tip them to a certain point (initial stability), but then the hull design works

Stability can be an important factor in big-water angling.

hard to keep you from tipping them much farther (secondary stability).

Sit-inside fishing kayaks are very stable, as well. I've suffered through many a boat wake from water-skiers and other powerboats that apparently thought more of my kayak's stability than I. My sit-inside never capsized, even in rough waves, wakes, and high wind when I was paddling hard to get back to a sheltered area or dry land. Sit-insides also have the added feature of being more wind-resistant due to their lower profile. That, coupled with the lower center of gravity, make the perceived stability on par with the actual stability. I've ridden waves in my SIK that, when I saw them coming, I thought I was doomed. After I'd survived, it seemed kind of fun. During the experience, however, "fun" was not one of the words I was uttering.

Though sit-on-top kayaks are often hailed for their stability, both types of boats—especially with today's modern hull designs—offer a safe day on the water. I'm not going to conclude this section by saying one is more stable than the other. I'm also not going to say that stability is overemphasized. Stability is important. And it's one of things that fishing kayaks—even the sleekest and fastest models—have built into their designs.

Is there a trade-off between stability and speed? Yes. Is there a trade-off between maneuverability and stability? Yes, there will be some. Boats that hang their hats on stability often are wider and heavier than their slightly less stable counterparts. Wider hulls mean more water resistance while you're paddling. It's simple physics. Long and sleek is fast. Fat and stubby will be less so. For fishing in sheltered areas and smaller waters, fat, stubby, and stable may be for you. If, however, you wind up as a tournament fisherman, or fish more frequently on large bodies of water, you may choose to compromise more to the speed end of the spectrum with a longer, narrower boat that is capable of keeping up with the competition. Stability, as mentioned previously, might be somewhat compromised, but that doesn't mean a faster boat will necessarily end with you getting wet. There's a lot to consider before making your final decision.

Is there a trade-off between stability and maneuverability? Yes, there will be some of that, too. In my small, ten-foot SIK, I can turn on a dime—and very quickly at that. In my first large, heavy SOT, I was surprised at the amount of effort it took to turn it around. This matters when fishing. Being able to quickly reposition or avoid water hazards is something to keep under consideration, especially when fishing the snag-filled areas that species like largemouth bass and pike and many other game fish inhabit. It's less important on big, open water. Like the stability differences between the two types of kayaks, though, it's something that you'll get used to. Even the lightest, nicest SOT kayaks lack a bit in the maneuverability department, but it's not an insurmountable problem.

I think anyone can get into an SIK and begin paddling fairly easily with a minimal amount of instruction or practice. SOTs, with their higher centers of gravity and angles of paddle attack, require slightly different techniques that may not seem quite as obvious as the common sense technique required to easily move an SIK. The different paddle attack for an SOT may add to the perceived instability until the technique is mastered.

So, which is more stable? Both types are stable.

A good, reputable kayak dealer will probably have a place for you to try out some boats. I've heard it said that you should never buy until you've tried. Good theory, but not always practical. You're likely to try an SIK and think, "Oh that's much easier and much more stable" than the SOT you just tried. It may *feel* that way, only because the SOT's learning curve is a bit steeper to reach the same comfort level. Like most things in life, you can adjust and become proficient with either. They all take practice. And when it comes to this sport, practice means "going fishing more often." Hard to argue with that.

Hardcore SOT guys will tell you that there's no comparison. SOTs are more stable. And the SIK crowd (though it's a much smaller crowd these days) will tell you that a good SIK is more stable than an equivalent SOT. To summarize, good angling kayaks will be stable by their very nature, no matter what you choose.

So, let's move on to other considerations before you make any decisions.

Weight

Let's talk about the physical attributes of the kayak itself. Weight and length are two characteristics that will help determine your

Visiting a reputable kayak dealer and doing your research are all part of the decision-making process.

choice of angling kayak. Weight is a primary concern because it influences your day on the water more than any other consideration. If you find yourself interested in a heavy kayak (my Ascend FS-128T sit-on-top, for example, is pushing one hundred pounds if the swivel seat is included in the weight), you'll need to keep a few things in mind. On the water, weight matters only in that it makes it slightly more difficult to get moving, and turning the boat from a dead stop is also more difficult. Long-distance paddling in a heavier kayak can cause more wear and tear on your body, as well. In the paddle selection (see page 80) and paddling chapters (see page 172), we'll discuss how some of this handicap can be ameliorated with the right paddle and paddling techniques.

Remember the early chapter of this book (see page 36) where I discussed snobbery and the high cost of high-end kayaks? Weight is the single biggest factor that the more expensive kayaks have over lesser-quality (and lower-cost) boats. Most of my kayaking is on a relatively sheltered, slow current creek, and my heavy Ascend is fine for that in every regard. On my forays out into larger bodies of water, where more long-distance paddling is required, the Ascend isn't ideal but—here's the thing—it's not that bad. I wouldn't use it for a very long-distance paddle, but it's certainly capable of almost everything the more expensive boats are. The lightest kayaks cost more. It's a simple truth. The heaviest ones, like mine, are often referred to as "barges" by their owners (and their detractors). But my barge is a fish-catching machine, and I don't ever feel undergunned competing with kayaks that cost twice as much. If it's a race to get to a fishing spot, then it would be an inferior craft. But the kind of fishing I enjoy is never a race. If you're a tournament fisherman, or plan on becoming one, you'll want to consider a lighter boat.

Where weight makes a huge difference is in portability—out of the water. We're going to talk about transporting your kayak in a subsequent chapter (see page 115), but since we're talking about weight, let's touch on it here. If you're going to cartop-carry your kayak, a heavy kayak isn't necessarily out of the question.

With the proper technique, you should be able to get an eighty-to one-hundred-pound kayak up on your roof yourself without too much difficulty if you're in good shape (or at least have no issues with your shoulders and back). Is it as easy as a fifty-pound kayak? No, of course not, but with good planning and the proper leverage, it is completely doable. Cartopping seems to be the most common means of kayak transportation these days, but there are other ways.

If you have a pickup truck, many kayaks can be carried in the bed, often with a tailgate extender. This eliminates the awkward overhead work, which is helpful when dealing with a heavy kayak. Finally, there are trailers. Both homemade trailers and those specifically designed for kayaks keep the boats very low during transport and make it easy to slide a heavy kayak off and into the water, or at least close to the water. A kayak cart can assist in longer drags down to the water. I had a kayak trailer before I had my heavy Ascend, and I have no trouble trailering the boat by myself. And, with the use of a cart, the weight melts away (more on that in a later chapter; see page 131).

The final consideration regarding weight is those times when you have to drag the kayak through mud, around obstacles, or through shallow stretches of water. Many anglers with heavier kayaks (and some with lighter ones) carry their two-wheeled kayak kart as an integral part of their fishing rig. That way they're never stuck with horsing the boat around unforeseen obstructions in the creek without some assistance. Kayaking can be a solitary sport, but if you regularly go with a partner or a spouse, having two people to load and carry the kayak can make all the difference in the world. I typically fish alone but have no problem with the heaviest kayak in my rotation.

Many kayaks come with carry handles. Sometimes these are well placed, and other times they're not. My kayaks are constantly being modified and upgraded, and aftermarket handles are one way to make your kayak moving challenges a little less daunting.

Light kayaks are great, if you can afford them. Sit-inside kayaks offer a lighter weight alternative to a heavy SOT if the weight factor figures heavily (see what I did there?) in your decision making. Heavy SOT kayaks are completely usable for all but the most expeditionary of kayak anglers, but they also sacrifice a bit in speed.

Get what you can afford, what you can handle, and whichever you will use more often.

Length

Angling kayaks come in a variety of lengths. A twelve-foot boat seems to be the standard length for most kayak fishing applications. It's at home in creeks, backwaters, ponds, and small lakes and is certainly suitable for larger waters. The length is short enough for easy maneuvering but long enough to improve tracking, or the

A big SOT is still at home on very small water.

ability of the boat to stay straight as you paddle. Fourteen-foot-plus boats are considered to be fairly large in the kayak-fishing world, but if your main focus is large lakes, open estuaries, or the ocean surf, the longer boat will likely be what you're looking for. What's gained in superior tracking and speed is lost in maneuverability, but when fishing open water, maneuverability is less a factor than speed. Large boats also make it somewhat easier to land the larger species that saltwater fishermen often encounter, and the same holds true for the large freshwater fish such as muskie and pike. If you're going to have a fifty-inch fish in your lap, the more room on the deck of your kayak, the better.

That brings me to what are considered the "short boats." My current SIK is a ten-foot Old Towne. I've read that ten-foot boats are excellent for small streams, ponds, and little else. Mine has been on enough small streams and lakes for me to verify that claim. However, it's also been on very big lakes (as in Great Lakes) and very big rivers (such as the Niagara River), and it performed well there, too. I still maintain that a ten- or twelve-foot SIK is an underrated fish-catching machine. They're maneuverable, can operate in scant inches of water, easily handle stiff currents, and are light enough and wind resistant enough to paddle all day without killing yourself.

Length does matter, but as in all aspects of fishing, much depends on the type of fishing you're planning to do and the body of water in which you plan to do it. I can promise you that within five years of reading this book, you probably will have several kayaks in your garage, of several different lengths, makes, types, and prices.

It's one of the joys of the sport.

Materials of Construction

This may be one attribute to which you pay little attention, but what it's made of is an essential piece of knowledge to tuck away if you're interested in the nuts and bolts of how your kayak was constructed and how that may affect its performance.

Most fishing kayaks are made from plastic polymer. The key item to look for during your kayak shopping and research is to see if the kayak is described as *rotomolded*. Rotomolding, in simple terms, means that the kayak is poured in multiple sections that are literally spun together to create what is essentially a single piece of plastic. Some lesser kayaks are glued or hot-joined together from separate sections. It's often at these joints that leakage (or worse, breakage) may occur. All you need to keep in mind is that if it says rotomolded, it's more likely a kayak that will last and cause you fewer problems. And, in a sport where many of your problems can occur in deep water, fewer problems are precisely what you want.

You'll hear me say this many times throughout this book, but kayak-fishing boats and equipment are evolving at such a rate that it's nearly impossible to keep up with each innovation.

Most kayaks are plastic, but other options are coming onto the market so frequently that by the time you read this, there may be a new standard. Other materials such as Kevlar and fiberglass are currently being used to produce new fishing kayaks. Each of these, like plastic polymer, will come with its own issues and strengths. For example, I'd hesitate to take a fiberglass kayak among the sunken boulders in my favorite stretch of steelhead stream, where I've bounced my heavy plastic kayak off rocks dozens of times with zero issues. Each material of construction that comes down the road is worthy of further research.

Comfort

Here's where the rubber meets the road—or at least where your posterior meets your kayak. Once again, in this category there is a clear winner. For all of my praise and devotion to sit-inside kayaks, for the most part they are not very comfortable. Sit-inside kayaks require you to sit in them. Obviously. Sitting in something that's already very low-profile requires you to sit nearly in the bottom of it. This leaves little room for a real seat. Some SIKs simply have a plastic molded seat built into the bottom. Others have a padded seat and backrest, but these are often very thin and uncomfortable. Some of the better SIKs offer a bit more high-tech seating.

SIK seats are generally lower and less comfortable than those on an SOT.

Aftermarket SIK seats can also be had for a reasonable price, but the more comfort and luxury afforded by the seat, the higher it tends to be. That, in turn, sacrifices that low center-of-gravity that is one of the stability cornerstones that makes SIKs appealing.

Sit-on-top kayaks often offer very good seating with webbed, ergonomic sling seats or lawn chair-type seats. My current SOT has a swivel seat to hang your feet over the edge in the warm water, or for better casting angles. Some adventurous kayak anglers have even installed larger bass boat seats for further comfort.

Another aspect in SIK discomfort is the closed cockpit. There's not much room to stretch your legs, or even bend them. An SOT allows full freedom of leg movement. Most of them offer enough deck room to wiggle around a little, even sit on the deck a bit so your rump has a change of scenery.

One of the things that surprises many anglers about their first time in an SOT is the fact that you get wetter. In warm weather

A typical SOT kayak seat, designed for comfort.

this is not a big deal, especially if you're wearing shorts and open shoes or bare feet. It can feel positively good! Unlike an SIK, in which your legs are covered by the cockpit roof, you *will* get water splashed on you from the paddle. The scupper holes will take care of the excess, but you should plan to get wet. This was a surprise to me, so don't let it be a surprise to you. In the heat of August you won't even notice, but in the cold of late November, you need to take it into consideration and take precautions. We will discuss clothing selection at length in a later chapter (see page 105), but for now keep in mind that there are clothes available that can keep cold weather SOT kayak fishing from being unbearable. Also, SOT kayaks expose your entire body to the elements. Again, this can be rectified with careful clothing choices, but many kayak anglers switch to their old SIKs when the weather really turns cold.

SIKs tend to be much drier, at least from the perspective that your legs rarely get soaked. SIKs get an "A" on the report card for protection against the elements, as well. But there's one final consideration that is sometimes the deal breaker for me. All kayaks get water in them, especially if it's raining or snowing, or you're angling in a particularly choppy surf. Kayak fishing will never be a 100 percent dry endeavor. However, the nice thing about an SOT kayak as opposed to the SIKs is that when water infiltrates an SIK, you're typically going to end up sitting in it. If you're quick with your bailer or sponge (my preference), you can keep from having *too much* water in the bottom of your boat, but you're going to have some. And it only takes a quarter inch of water to make your day miserable if you're sitting in it. The raised seats more closely associated with sit-on-top kayaks will keep your butt out of the water. Simple as that. Take it from someone who has spent hours with wet pants, tolerating it just because the fish were biting; it's much better to have your shorts stay dry in the first place. SOTs win this one.

Aside from comfort against the elements, the ability to move around, and the scourge of water infiltration in SIKs, there's one last comfort consideration: the low "slumped" posture created by an SIK can cause back fatigue in a few short hours. Very rare is the fishing day in my SIK that I don't feel the need to paddle the boat to the bank, get out, and walk around a bit. It's not just the posture, it's the restriction of blood flow by having your legs out in front of you and level with your hips. There's real medical science involved here, but simply put, your body is just not made to sit that way. In a sit-on-top, your legs are still out in front of you, but at a lower level. This is a much more natural position for your body's blood flow. Combined with the added benefit of a more ergonomic seat and back and the fact that you can shift and squirm around a bit, the SOT makes for a much more comfortable ride. I can spend hours and hours in my SOT without needing a break. And, with a stand-up model, if you need to stand up—you just stand up! No break needed.

SOTs win hands-down in the comfort department. If you're never going fishing for more than an hour or two, or never plan to

SIKs offer more protection from the elements but fewer storage options.

spend the entire day in the boat, this may not matter to you. But to many of us, when we get a day to fish, we like to take advantage of every last minute—often from dawn to dusk with barely a stop for a bathroom break. Why not do it in as much comfort as is possible in a small plastic boat? Sit-on-top for the win.

Storage

This one is also not much of a contest. Sit-inside kayaks typically limit the amount of gear that can be brought along. Though there's usually a fair amount of space for a good-sized tackle box under the cockpit and a tank well on the back for carrying additional gear, fishing from an SIK generally means limiting the amount of gear you may bring along. There's a lot that can be done to modify an SIK to carry more gear. The old standard "crate" in the rear tank well can hold a lot of gear, as well as dry bags placed in the cockpit. With some careful rigging (see page 223), there's potential for arranging the deck in front of the cockpit for additional tie-downs and storage. The problem with additional gear in an SIK, however, is often the ability to reach it. Limited movement, due to the confines of the cockpit, prevent long reaches for gear without compromising stability. There's not a whole lot of crawling around for gear in an SIK. If you can't reach it from your seated position, you're sunk. Perhaps that's a poor choice of words in a kayak fishing book, but it's something to consider.

Sit-on-top kayaks excel in the storage department. They win this division, hands-down. If you're looking to cart as much gear in your angling kayak as a tournament bass fisherman might, SOTs are for you. Most tournament kayak fishermen carry a lot of gear, and most of them will be found in a sit-on-top kayak. A typical SOT might have a couple of dry storage hatches within reach of the seat, and another couple at opposite ends of the boat. Due to the open floor plan of a sit-on-top kayak, it's possible to carefully move around a bit on the deck to reach the gear in the far compartments,

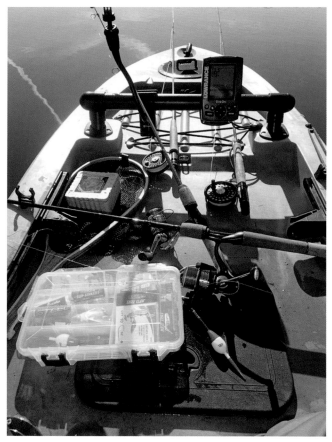

The open floor plan and multiple storage compartments offer many options for anglers who don't feel the need to oversimplify.

as well. When we talk later in the book about adding gadgets and especially electronics to the boat, the additional storage space in the hollow hull design of an SOT makes a convenient place for storing batteries and running wires. In addition to the normal fishing crate for those frequently needed accessories, there's usually also room for a bait bucket, something that can't typically be used in an SIK, for the most part. This may not be an important consideration to some, but for others the ability to fish with live bait is an important part of the package.

As stated earlier in the book, an enjoyable part of kayak fishing is the ability—and the need—to simplify things a bit. Anyone who is passionate about anything has likely amassed a good deal of paraphernalia to enhance the enjoyment of the hobby. If you like the idea of slimming down your fishing gear selection, either type of kayak will work well for you. However, if you're one of those people that has to have every last size and color of every last lure? SOT is the only good answer.

Me? I have both.

Accessories

Fishermen love gadgets. I'm probably more of a holdout than a lot of my friends, since I still maintain that flyfisherman mentality about carrying only what you need. More recently, though, I've gotten sucked in, at least when it comes to kayak fishing. My current SOT is starting to look (*gulp*) like a modern bass boat in miniature. Theoretically, both SIKs and SOTs can be outfitted with nearly identical accessories. Each can take above-deck rod holders, flush-mount rod holders, electronics, gear crates, tackle boxes, lights, and just about everything else you can imagine.

It may just be a mental block with me, but I'm more inclined to keep my SIK simple, since it represents the beginning of my kayak-fishing career. It was a time when I *did* keep things simple and more streamlined. My SOT, since the first day I had it, seems to be an experiment in excess. I just finished building mounting bars for lights, cameras, GPS, and fish-finding gear. It looks pretty spiffy compared to the SIK, but in reality, I could have added all of that gear to my SIK, too.

The only advantage held by the sit-on-top in this regard is the below-deck storage capability mentioned earlier in this chapter. Batteries and wires can be easily secured below deck, out of the way and out of sight. The truth of the matter, though, is that waterproof battery boxes and wires can also be stuffed up in the cockpit recesses of an SIK, as well.

There's also the added advantages of SOTs having more perfectly flat surfaces on which to mount gear and electronics. Even with the rounder, more aerodynamic hulls of a typical sit-inside kayak, however, there's always a way.

Kayak fishermen are, almost to a person, very inventive. If it can be done, we will find a way to do it. I've come up with a few contraptions on my own that I didn't find in a book or a Google search. Figuring out ways to accessorize your boat is one of the great things about this sport. The birth of the kayak-fishing age coinciding with the golden age of the Internet means that there are unlimited resources and ideas for you to try. In the end, you can copy others' ideas all you want when it comes to accessorizing, but don't be afraid to strike out on your own. You might just think of the next big thing.

So which is easier to accessorize? SIT? SOK? I call this one a tie.

The Body Factor

I'm not a big guy (5' 9"), but I'm not a skinny guy, either. I can comfortably fit in an SIK or SOT. If you're much bigger than that, I would suggest an SOT, just for their roominess. SIKs limit legroom, and if you're sporting a really big pair of legs, you might find yourself a bit cramped. SOTs typically have a higher weight rating than SIKs, though they can vary widely from brand to brand and model to model. They're a good starting point at which to make a solid decision. Keep in mind that with an SOT and its additional storage, you're more likely to load it down with gear, and if you're a gear-hound, it's not difficult to add a *lot* of weight. All of this needs to be taken into account when purchasing your kayak. It's very useful to do an Internet search looking for what large-sized anglers have had to say about the models of kayak that you are considering. There's nothing embarrassing in learning that the kayak you're interested in might actually be a little bit tight for your body type. Better to figure that out now than the first time you try out the kayak and realize that you've made a mistake. Better yet, try sitting in one and see how it feels before taking it home.

Conversely, if you're a very small person, you may find that paddling a twelve- or thirteen-foot SOT is simply too hard for you. It's not for everyone. If it's difficult, you are not going to enjoy it. Find a boat that suits you, and just as I advise the larger people reading this book to do, look for reviews suggesting which kayak might be better suited to *your* size.

Physical abilities are another consideration. Kayaking and kayak fishing are physical sports. As we'll talk about later in the paddling chapters (starting on page 172), *you are the motor* on this fishing boat. Of course (at the risk of sounding like a pharmaceutical advertisement), if you're suffering from any disease that the stress of exercise might exacerbate, you should consult with your doctor before undertaking this adventure. Kayak paddling, especially if you find yourself in heavy current or caught out in the wind and fighting to get back to shore, can be a physical challenge. For the most part, I fish calm waters and mild currents. The exercise associated with kayaking is pleasant and mild, relaxing and enjoyable. There have been moments, though, when a stiff wind came out of nowhere, threatening to take me out to sea, and I had to work my ass off to get home. Your heart will be pounding. Your arms will get tired. It may never happen to you, but, then again, it might unless you completely restrict yourself to small, sheltered waterways and ponds. You need to ask yourself (and your doctor) if you're up to this sport. That being said, the exercise inherent in kayak fishing is a great way to *get* in shape, not only physically, but mentally. I've never come home from a day of kayak fishing more stressed than when I left. That reduction in stress alone is good for the body. The exercise is a bonus.

WHAT COLOR?

I'm not going to belabor this point because on its face, honestly, it seems kind of silly to me. I could sum this whole section up by saying, "Just get whatever damn color you want." Believe it or not, however, there are factions of the kayak angling community that think this is a big deal. For some applications, I can see their point. Currently, the debate in kayak color rages mainly around safety. Kayaks are a low-profile watercraft. Even the biggest kayak's profile is a slim wedge against the distant horizon at best, invisible at worst, especially during choppy water conditions. On large bodies of water, visibility to other boats is a concern. Big boats run into other big boats all the time. Collisions with kayaks are not unheard of. There have been several high-profile fatal accidents, including one involving a group of kayak fishermen, several of whom were killed by a single powerboat.

There are sloppy boaters out there, just like there are sloppy drivers on the highway. Maintaining high visibility in the water is an important part of kayak fishing in busy waterways. Most fishing kayaks these days are either high visibility (red, yellow, or some combination of the two) or, at the opposite end of the spectrum, drab or even camouflage colored.

I'm sure this will not sit well with some, but I prefer drab and dark colors. For me, the important aspect of a fishing kayak is the *fishing* part. I fish mostly in shallow-water environments, but I also spend a fair amount of time on clear, deep lakes. I feel that the drab colors will have less of an impact on spooking fish. Maybe it's my deer and duck hunting background, but my assumption is that if you're paddling around in a natural-toned kayak, it might be a

The author's preference in kayaks tends toward drab, natural colors.

bit less off-putting than a bright yellow one. Again, check those magazine covers. Yellow seems to be the "proteam" option these days, but I don't subscribe. Perhaps if I spent more time in the open ocean or miles out on the open Great Lakes, I might consider a more vivid color. But I *do* spend time out on the big, open water, and I don't feel the need for a brightly colored boat. You might. If you're concerned about busy waterways and visibility, maybe the brightly colored boats that seem to be overtaking the drab boats in popularity *are* for you. If, however, you're more of an earth-tone type whose attire and sensibilities tend more toward flannel and camo, there are other things you can do to increase visibility. Later on, we're going to talk about rigging your boat with lights for low-light fishing (see page 203), as well as putting up a small flag that can be seen above all but the highest waves (see page 199). Both of these are good ideas, regardless of the color of your boat.

Some anglers prefer high visibility colors for safety reasons.

If you're into looking stealthy, get camo or drab. If you're into the bright and flashy hot rod colors that seem to increasingly be the colors of choice for fishing kayaks, get one of those. If you're desperately worried about being seen by other boats, bright is the way to go. Keep in mind, however, that you can increase your visibility by getting paddles with high-contrast ends and wear brightly colored clothing, as well. If you're equally afraid of scaring fish in heavily fished areas of low or clear water, go drab or camo.

No, I'm not making your mind up for you.

ALTERNATE PROPULSION OPTIONS

This section is going to be purposely short. There's a growing segment of the kayak fishing community that considers kayaks propelled by alternate propulsion (that is to say anything other than a paddle) as not engaging in true kayak fishing. I'm not going to go that far. Do what you want. Live and let live. Fish and let fish. Some individuals consider anything other than paddle propulsion to be an affront to the sport. Some kayak anglers are perfectly fine with a pedal-powered boat but draw the line at the addition of a trolling motor. The choice is yours. I've seen the very cool YouTube videos of the crazy rigs some fishermen have come up with to use an electric trolling motor to move their boat through the water. Pedal-powered kayaks (there are three manufacturers that offer pedal power as of this writing, probably ten by tomorrow) also have their aficionados. If that's the way you're leaning, you've probably already researched far beyond the scope of anything I can present to you in this book. But, if you're just getting started in the sport (as I suspect many readers of this book may be), you might be thinking, "Hmm, sometime down the road, I might want to try that out." Therefore, we'll briefly cover these two modes of propulsion, so you have the information in hand before your first kayak purchase.

Pedal Power

Pedal-powered kayaks are cool. I was sucked in early by the pedal-powered phenomenon. I soon learned that the realities of pedal power versus paddle power often belie the hype surrounding them. Your legs are more powerful than your arms, so pushing your kayak through the water with leg power makes sense. Indeed, you've probably seen the GoPro videos of pedal kayaks slicing effortlessly through the water at a rate of speed a paddling kayak angler could only hope to attain. It's true. Pedaling a kayak moves it quickly through the water. But at what sacrifice?

Funny you should ask that. There are many sacrifices. Maneuverability must be taken into consideration. Pedal power has only the ability to move you forward and backward. Turning, therefore, relies on a rudder that must still be controlled by hand, or, in some instances, a paddle is used to assist in turning. Stability is undoubtedly the biggest sacrifice. Your legs are constantly in motion during forward pedaling. While paddling aids in balancing the unstable craft (all kayaks are more unstable than other fishing boats), pedaling does not allow the widespread balancing that paddling enhances. The position you maintain in the boat must be rigidly maintained throughout the pedaling exercise. This often causes a condition that sit-inside kayak fishermen refer to as "yak-back." It's a painful, numbing condition. I've experienced it on many occasions. Unlike the paddler, the pedaler cannot shift positions to attain a more comfortable one during movement. You'll get there faster, but your back is going to hurt more. It's not a trade-off that I consider worthwhile.

If you think I'm just trashing pedal-powered 'yaks, I'm not. They serve their purpose for many anglers, especially in large, open-water applications. Many of us, however, don't strictly fish in large, open water. Pedal power, due to the construction of the propellers, eliminates some of the shallow-water ability found in paddle-only kayaks. The pedal drives hang down, hit rocks, and— all too often—gather weeds and other foliage. I've heard this called "harvesting seaweed." I harvest enough with my fishing lures and my paddle. I don't need to add a combine to my kayak. Most of the fishiest places I fish would make a pedal-powered craft an impossibility due to the vegetation and underwater obstacles that present little or no problem to a more traditional paddle-powered kayak.

With pedal gears, pedals, and rudders, additional weight is added to the kayak. This additional weight is a consideration when hoisting the kayak onto your transportation racks, as well as the consideration of damaging the pedal-drive or rudder while dragging it around shallow water obstacles.

By now, you think I *hate* pedal-powered kayaks. I don't. They do serve their purpose on large water where obstacles are few and when portaging around (or paddling through) shallow water is not an issue. They can cover water more quickly than any SOT or SIK, for sure, but when covering large water means a sacrifice in stability, you have to ask yourself if it's worth it. For a beginning kayak angler, I don't recommend the pedal-powered boats. There will be time for more kayaks down the road, and, as mentioned earlier, I promise that you'll end up with a few of them in the next few years. Maybe one of them will be a pedal-powered craft. For now, my recommendation is a paddle-powered SOT or SIK to get you started in this sport. Don't sacrifice weight, maneuverability, or stability just to have something in which you can move across water very quickly. If that's your goal, maybe you should be considering a powerboat. That brings us to the next section.

Motorizing Your Kayak

There are a lot of DIY kayak fishermen out there who have invented very interesting ways to add an electric motor (or even a low-horse-power gas motor) to their fishing kayaks. The Internet is loaded with these kayaks and their funky powered add-ons. Maybe you're getting a fishing kayak so you add a motor to it. Right now, there are a couple of manufacturers that are designing kayaks with electric drive systems built right in. I wonder, "Why buy a kayak at all?" But that's me, and don't let me stop you from following your crazy dreams. However, let me just touch on a few quick points before you decide on a kayak based on how well it will accept a motor (and there are many coming on the market with hulls designed specifically to accept an electric motor).

Kayaks are inherently more unstable than powered boats. As mentioned in the pedal-power section above, the kayak relies on the paddler to maintain stability. When you add a motor, even just a large trolling motor that is capable of moving the boat along at impressive speeds, stability is the first and most important sacrifice. Oh, hell yes, that boat will go through the water like a dream, but turning too sharply or (God forbid) running quickly over a submerged obstacle will turn your fishing day into a bad day very quickly. Paddling allows great control over anything you might encounter in the water. A motor added to your kayak removes some of that control. If you've ever run up on a submerged log or rock while paddling, you know how quickly things can go bad. Imagine the stress of doing that under power, and perhaps having the control ripped from your hand. There's a greater likelihood of ending up in the drink when putting electrical or gas power to a kayak. Kayaks really are capable of very good speed in the water without the addition of a motor.

If that's not enough reason for you to first consider paddling before you consider adding motorized hardware to your kayak, keep this in mind: like the pedal-powered kayaks, the addition of an electric trolling motor or small gas motor decreases your ability to fish in (or traverse through, on your way to deeper water) very shallow water. I've found the ability to fish in shallow water or access thick vegetation to be the number one criterion that has made me a true believer in kayak fishing. I rarely worry about submerged obstacles, shallow weed beds, or boulder fields. I just fish. If you're powered by even a small electric motor, enjoying that same ability means raising the propeller unit out of the muck. This is not as easily accomplished in a small kayak as it is in a more stable powered fishing boat.

Finally, before we move on to the next chapter of the book, keep in mind that many kayak angling clubs disallow powered craft for their fishing tournaments. The thought process may be that motors offer an unfair advantage, though I'm not so sure that is true for all of the reasons listed above.

WHAT'S GOING TO WORK FOR YOU?

I've given you the basics surrounding the criteria for selecting your kayak. You should take that information and apply it to the kind of fishing *you* will be doing. Will you leisurely be paddling down a secluded stream, jumping out now and then to wade and cast? Will you be plowing across whitecaps on Lake Ontario, trying to reach seventy feet of water where the lake trout have been biting this week? Maybe you're just going to limit yourself to a small, calm lake and only fish once or twice a month. Do you need a fast boat? A stable boat? Do you need to compromise one for the other? Do you need to carry a lot of gear, or are you happy being a minimalist? Is a heavy boat okay, or do you need something you can easily throw on top of your 1996 Ford Escort?

This is information only you can answer. Every angling kayak purchase will entail a bit of compromise. The decision making can be confusing, but the research and anticipation can also be a part of the fun. Use what you've learned here to make the best decision you can, based on your needs and (of course) your budget.

Good luck!

To Rudder or Not to Rudder

The question posed in the title of this chapter could easily be asked in the previous chapter on kayak selection, or the later chapter on angling kayak rigging (see page 223). It's not an easy one to answer. However, given the assumption that since you're reading this book, you are not already deep into the art and science of kayak fishing, I'll give you my short answer, and that is *not to rudder*. I must qualify that by saying not right away.

To establish the stability and size that equate with a safe and comfortable day on the water, modern SOT kayaks have sacrificed in other ways, as we've already discussed. Even the best SOTs won't be as maneuverable or as fast as an SIK. They won't track as well, especially in wind and waves. You'll read a lot of opinions, especially from ocean-going kayak anglers, that insist a rudder is a must-have. You'll even read from large lake kayak fishermen that a rudder is an absolute must.

Not so fast.

Rudders can add tracking ability in stiff wind and high waves. I'm not going to debate that. However, they also have some downsides. They're expensive, for one. Even a DIY kit can run into the hundreds of dollars. Also, they put additional hardware on deck with ropes, lines, controls, and the rudder mount itself. This is additional weight that affects carrying the 'yak overland, as well as paddling it on the water. Most kayak anglers, even if it's only during launch and landing, find themselves in very shallow water. This is true for small pond fishermen and those crazy nuts who hit the ocean in hopes of landing a three-hundred-pound tuna on their angling kayak. The rudder can add to the innate difficulty of launching and landing a kayak, even under the most ideal circumstances. And for those of us freshwater anglers who spend most of our time in just a few feet of water? The rudder is a seaweed and submerged limb magnet.

Do I seem antirudder? I am, just a bit, only because it erodes that simplicity that I feel should be the basis of good kayak angling.

Sunrise off the bow of the author's SOT.

It's just one more thing to go wrong, in short. Cables can break, for example. Can a rudder solve your kayak's poor tracking? Sure. It can help. But it's not magic. Will it assist when you're stuck trying to get back to shore in a following wind? Maybe. But does that make it worth the fifteen pounds of milfoil it will pick up in your favorite shallow water spot that you frequent far more often than the open expanses? In my humble opinion, no. But, again, that's just my opinion. Like everything else in regard to kayak angling, to rudder or not to rudder is a personal choice. If you're going to spend most of your time on the open ocean, or deep Great Lakes, it can be a help. It can also be a hindrance to launching, landing, and carrying, as well as one more technological issue that you will have to deal with.

I'd suggest going rudderless for your first few outings. If you purchased a bargain-basement kayak that won't track worth a damn, or if you find yourself fishing only in the deep, open water where the rudder's presence would only be an asset instead of a problem, you may elect to add a rudder at some point. But you don't need it right away. This is a choice that can be put off a bit, and I recommend holding off on this expensive and sometimes cumbersome addition until you are absolutely certain that you need it.

Choosing a Paddle

Your kayak is your fishing boat. Unlike other fishing boats, *you are the motor.* Your arms, your back, your enthusiasm, and your style all determine what kind of motor you are. But there is a single selection you can make early on that will determine how efficient a motor you are: your paddle.

I'm going to make an educated prediction: you just spent somewhere between three hundred and two thousand dollars on your new kayak. Whether it was an online purchase or carefully selected from the expansive racks of a reputable kayak dealer after careful testing and under the guidance of an expert salesperson, your next decision will be the paddle. Having shelled out some big cash already, you are probably considering a cheap paddle. By cheap, I mean a paddle for fifty or sixty dollars. It's probably aluminum, maybe plastic. You still need to buy a personal flotation device (PFD, as we'll discuss in the next chapter starting on page 91) and maybe a fish finder. Perhaps you'll want to add a different rod holder or two, and an anchor trolley. Oh, that's right, you'll need to buy an anchor, too . . . The numbers start adding up in your head and you start to panic. After all, you'll definitely need

Choosing the correct paddle is an important decision.

some money left over to add a few new rods and beef up your tackle box for the inaugural kayak-fishing expedition. You reach for the cheap paddle and pull out your credit card.

Wait. Don't do it! At least not until you read this section.

Let's take the basic paddle that most of us start with—the aluminum kayak paddle. It's serviceable. It isn't going to break very easily. It's economical. You think that sixty dollars is a lot to pay for that paddle, and sixty bucks *is* sixty bucks. But is that aluminum paddle the best for you? If you're shopping a discount outdoor store or on a big-box online store, that's the paddle that jumps out at you. It *will* work. It *is* affordable. It's also heavy and there are a lot more options than aluminum, in a variety of shapes and sizes that are worth exploring. If you're in a hurry, and your checking account is pretty well drained from the kayak purchase, check the size chart, grab the aluminum paddle, and head for the water. It will work fine for you. As stated early in this book, you don't need the best of the best of everything to enjoy kayak fishing. Chances are, though, you'll eventually be back at the paddle rack, especially if you find yourself loving the sport and delving more deeply into kayak gear than you originally predicted. When you *do* decide to rethink that first aluminum paddle, here's what you should keep in mind.

MATERIALS OF CONSTRUCTION

Let's start with the one you're most likely to buy (or have already bought): aluminum. It's very tough. My aluminum paddle has been through hell. It's been used to push off rocks and used to pole through mucky marshes. It has also been used to fend off geese and swans, and, more than once, it saved me from falling into the drink when exiting or entering my kayak when I jammed it into the bank. I haven't tried to break my aluminum paddle, and I'm not so sure that would be easy to do. What the aluminum construction has in strength and durability, it gives up in weight. This may not mean much to you at first, but it will eventually. A heavy paddle can be taxing on the arms during long paddles and has the unfortunate characteristic of conducting cold temperatures under cold conditions. Aluminum can be hard on the hands. Of course, paddling gloves can be a work-around. But I don't know many fishermen who enjoy fishing with gloved hands. Aluminum is fine for most paddlers, but it is not the best option. One of the first things my friend, and kayak angling guru, Randy Bergin said to me when we fished together was, "We've gotta get you a better paddle." I didn't think much of it then; I do now.

The next material we'll look at is plastic. There are bargain basement plastic paddles and more expensive versions made from higher quality plastic. Doing your research on specific paddles is a must. Some plastics are absolute junk, and others are actually a step up from aluminum. You have to do your homework. The durability and weight of these paddles varies widely. A good assumption with plastic paddles is that you *will* get what you pay for. Plastic is typically fairly tough and does not transmit cold to the hands like aluminum. I personally don't feel very good about going out on the water with a paddle that may not get me home. We'll talk about backup plans for losing your paddle later in the book, but losing one is different from *breaking* one. As for weight, plastic paddles also vary widely. All will be at least slightly lighter than an aluminum paddle.

Finally, let's talk about carbon fiber or carbon composite. Carbon fiber is strong, light, and durable. You'll often see carbon fiber paddles listed as carbon *composite*. Typically (not always—this is another aspect of kayaking that is constantly evolving), carbon composite is a mixture of fiberglass and carbon fiber. For the purposes of this section, when I say "carbon," I'm referring both to carbon fiber and carbon composite paddles. Is it as durable as aluminum? No, not likely. But it will survive all of the abuses listed above and, with reasonable care, will last every bit as long. It doesn't transmit cold to the hands. Carbon's selling point to kayak enthusiasts—and kayak fishermen in particular—is its weight. This is something you need to experience in person. Even if you prefer to do all your shopping online, treat yourself to a trip to a nicer kayak shop and compare an aluminum paddle to a carbon fiber paddle. You'll quickly see there is no comparison. Carbon is ridiculously light. If Randy hadn't handed me his carbon paddle to compare to my aluminum one that morning out on the water, I might never have switched. Now, it's safe to say, I'll never switch back to aluminum.

Does weight matter, or is it just a luxury to have a space-age, lightweight paddle? That depends. The reason kayak fishermen are flocking to carbon paddles is the nature of the kayak itself. Fishing kayaks are typically wider and heavier than most recreational kayaks, as discussed earlier. It takes a bit more force to get a fishing kayak moving than a more streamlined touring kayak. This is where the idea of a lighter paddle matters. Not strictly for comfort and reduction of arm fatigue, a lighter paddle makes it *easier* to apply greater force to move a kayak through the water.

Some common wisdom out there (I've seen it repeated ad nauseam on kayak fishing forums and blogs online) is that you

Which is the correct paddle for you?

should focus your money on the best paddle you can get, even if it means buying a lesser boat. I'm not in this camp at all. I say get the boat you want (and can afford), and then get the best paddle that *fits within your budget.* Carbon paddles run the gamut from a hundred dollars and change all the way up to five or six hundred dollars. Could I afford a five-hundred-dollar paddle? I don't know, but I'm not doing it. I didn't pay five hundred dollars for my first fishing *kayak.* There are some great paddles out there that are much more affordable that still give you the light weight and added power that our heavy fishing kayaks require. I have a friend with a five-hundred-dollar paddle. It's great. Light, efficient. And . . . *he's afraid to take it out and break it.* He'll only use it on open water for fear of wrecking it on a boulder or some other submerged object in the tight confines sometimes found while creek fishing. Is that paddle worth five hundred dollars? Not if you won't use it.

PADDLE LENGTH

Any kayak shop or website will give you a chart to help you determine what length of kayak paddle shaft you should purchase. These charts vary slightly but are created on tried-and-true principles based on the height of the paddler and the width of the kayak. For my first fishing kayak, I consulted a chart and bought a paddle. It was too short. It happens. Though other experts may regale you with detailed formulas for kayak paddle selection, there are a few things you should keep in mind. One chart, for example, says that if I'm 5' 9" and the kayak is 33 inches wide, I need a 240-cm paddle (don't get me started on the metric system, but that's how paddles are measured). Well . . . sure. That formula worked for my sit-inside kayak. But for my sit-on-top, it has an adjustable seat that can be quite a bit higher than an SIK's seat, even in its lowest position. In its upper seat position, that 240-cm paddle seemed like it could barely reach the water. I bought a 250-cm, and it made all the difference. That's right: ten centimeters made a lot of difference. That longer paddle also works equally well in smaller boats, I was surprised to learn. I'm far from a paddle expert, but in my opinion, for a large kayak-fishing boat, you almost can't go too long with a paddle. Others may disagree, but I'm telling you my firsthand experiences.

SHAFT

Most kayak fishermen I've observed use a straight-shaft paddle. My assumption is that's because the straight-shaft paddles are more readily available in the variety of materials we've discussed above. There are, however, bent-shaft paddles. These can increase efficiency, especially when working from the raised seat position of an SOT fishing kayak. The bent shaft also has the added benefit of staying in place better on your lap when you drop the paddle to fight a fish. Trust me, even though your kayak comes with paddle holders and/or clips, your paddle is going to spend a *lot* of time in your lap. Though straight-shaft still seems to be the industry standard, bent-shaft (or crankshaft, as they're sometimes called) may be something for you to consider.

BLADE SHAPE AND SIZE

This is an area that can get unnecessarily complicated for the first-time kayak angler, but there are a few simple concepts to grasp when looking at those funny things at each end of the paddle—the blades. Blades have a characteristic that is commonly referred to as *bite.* Simply put, that's how the blade engages (or bites) the water. Sparing you the science involved so neither of us gets bored, bite matters in that the more of it you have, the more efficiently your blade will engage the water and push the kayak forward. "Slip" is another characteristic you'll hear described by the experts. Just think of slip as the opposite of bite. With a big, heavy boat loaded with lots of fishing gear, you want more bite and less slip. It's that simple. Now, how do we get it?

Blade size is one way to better engage the water. It's common sense, but the larger the blade, the more *oomph* (bite) you are going to get with each paddle stroke. For big, burly fishermen in big, burly boats, big blades are the way to go. You'll accelerate more quickly, turn more easily, and you'll also find it easier on those days you're battling wind and current. But, as stated at the beginning of this chapter, *you are the motor* that moves those paddles that move that kayak. If you are a very small person with a relatively small and light boat, you may find a blade that's too large to be fatiguing, since you'll be working a bit harder on each stroke. This is one of those instances that can be trial and error, and there's no substitute for trying a few different paddle sizes. Generally, most kayak fishermen like bigger paddle blades. The downside to large blades? At cruising speed, the larger blades are not as easy to maintain speed due to their water displacement. A touring kayak enthusiast would want a smaller blade. But for fishing, with its frequent stopping and starting, the power inherent in a larger blade is worth the tradeoff, particularly when regularly jumping from one honey hole to the next.

Blade *shape* is an important factor when selecting paddles. Unless you've been kayaking or kayak fishing a while, it's probably something you never considered. A long, thin blade will result in a weaker bite. A squarer (stubbier) blade will give you more bite. Remember, the more bite, the more quickly you'll get moving through the water. A cupped blade (or spoon-shaped) will have more bite than a flat-profile blade. Most kayak blades on the market (and all of those that I own) have a slightly cupped shape.

Blade *thickness* has some effect on paddling efficiency, as well. The thickness will be dependent on the materials of construction as well as the specific paddle design. In simple terms, a thin blade (much like a sharp knife) will engage the water more quickly than a thick (or dull) blade. These few millimeters may not seem like much, but the ability of the paddle to *fall* into the water as opposed to the added effort of having to *push* it into the water will result in less fatigue over a long day paddling. The difference between a thick and a thin paddle blade will be very obvious the first time you compare them.

Finally, there are a couple of paddles out there that are being marketed specifically to kayak anglers. One of these designs incorporates a notch in the top of the paddle purportedly to assist in getting snagged lures out of weeds. Great concept, right? Well . . . I thought so, too. While the notched paddles work for retrieving lures, they cause another problem—with paddling! The notches are notoriously good at picking up weeds and debris from the surface of the water. I've heard more than one angler complain about them. In weedy areas, the notched blades become a true nuisance. And in nonweedy areas and deep water? You aren't going to be retrieving a lure on your 240-cm paddle in fifty feet of water. Just a word of caution. It's a nice concept, but . . .

A NOTE ON FLEXIBILITY

Some paddles come with adjustable ferrules. The ability to adjust the length of the paddle can be particularly handy in a fishing kayak when fishing from different seat height adjustments. A higher seat while you're fishing? You can make the paddle longer. Wish to move the seat down for some long-distance paddling? Make the paddle shorter.

Similarly, another adjustment that many (even inexpensive) paddles have is the ability to *feather*. Feathering, simply put, is rotating the paddle so the two blades are at a different angle to each other. Touring kayak enthusiasts will often feather their paddles anywhere from forty-five degrees up to sixty or even seventy. This prevents wrist fatigue over long paddles and can help paddling

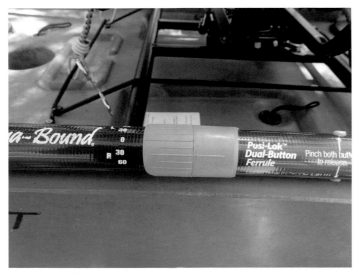

This paddle can be "feathered" to suit your paddling style.

efficiency based on your paddling style and skill level. I prefer to have my paddles along the same plane. That is just how I learned to do it, and I can't get comfortable with a feathered paddle. Others with whom I fish regularly have their paddles feathered to fit their style of paddling. It's a matter of preference, and since most paddles are easily adjustable, it's something you can take your time and figure out on the water. What you should keep in mind now, however, is that it might suit you in the future to buy a paddle now that is feathering-capable. Most are.

IN SUMMATION

I'm not going to change my tune from the earlier chapter in this book where I suggested that you not be sucked in by feeling like you have to buy the highest-dollar equipment on the market. The same holds true for paddles. You can get by with a cheap paddle, but a few more dollars will get you something that might work a little better for you. To me, a decent paddle is a good investment. You'll save in fatigue and discomfort (especially in cold temperatures and on long excursions), and, most important, your paddle is the one piece of equipment other than your kayak that you need to stay working in order to get you safely home to your family. Breaking the bank is not necessary for a good paddle, but, if you're going to really skimp on costs, your paddle may not be the item on which to do it.

Author with large, male bowfin.

Choosing (and Using) Your Personal Flotation Device

You've got your kayak selected, or at least you have a pretty good idea of where you're going with that decision. You've thought about your paddle a bit, and maybe it is (that magical term) "out for delivery." It's all very exciting, so let's get real for a minute. If you've skimmed through this book at all and looked at the pictures (spoiler alert!), you've seen some photos of your intrepid author and his family and acquaintances doing the "grip and grin" (trophy fish photo) without a personal flotation device. I considered leaving out those photos. I'm not proud of them (except for some of the fish). I've been canoeing, boating, and kayaking for my whole life. Forty years or better. The days I've spent on the water *not* strapped into a personal flotation device outnumber the days I have. It's a simple truth, and that's why I'm not pretending it's not true. I'm still here to tell about it. Am I fortunate or just plain stupid? That's up to you to decide. I'm going with stupid and fortunate.

During one of my earliest real adventures in my friend's canoe, we capsized in the icy waters of a Lake Ontario tributary in March in moderate current. Frank scrambled quickly and made it to the bank—it was only a few feet of water. Fearing that we'd be in deep trouble if we lost the old Coleman canoe, I grabbed the stern handle and stood in the current, hanging on for dear life. In the few seconds it took Frank to run down the bank and help me drag the submerged canoe to the edge, my legs numbed completely and I couldn't move. Had Frank not been within easy reach of me, and able to pull me to dry land, I would have died. Period. At thirteen years old, I would have been dead and gone. The deep pools a few hundred yards below me would have swallowed my body, and I wouldn't have been found without dragging the bottom.

Melodramatic much? You decide.

I could tell you in most of the photos, I was in two feet of water, and the temps were above seventy degrees. That's true. Much of my fishing is in a relatively shallow creek. But not *all* of those photos depict me in the safest possible conditions. Some of those photos show me kayaking in thirty feet of water, with a chill both above and below the surface. That said, temperature is not the only deciding factor in the importance of selection and use of a personal flotation device. The simple fact of the matter, to paraphrase an article I read on kayak safety a couple of years ago, is this: *You can't swim when you're unconscious.*

People die in big boats every year. Even the largest fishing kayaks are not big boats. I'm a very strong swimmer and always held in the back of my mind that if I couldn't get back into my capsized kayak (something we'll discuss later in the safety section, see page 145), I would simply swim the kayak back to shore. I always *carried* a PFD on board my boats and kayaks but rarely used it, except in some bass tournaments (on a full-sized bass boat) when running from fishing spot to fishing spot. The truth of the matter is that it's very unlikely that you'll need a PFD. The same could be said of seat belts. But, like seat belts, the day you need a PFD and aren't wearing one, its absence could very well mean the difference between life and death.

Many kayakers die in the water every year. Is it because of temperature? Sure. It happens. One guy was kayak fishing in Lake Erie this November and died. He had on his PFD but wasn't dressed appropriately for the chance of capsizing in frigid water. He succumbed to hypothermia before he could be rescued (we'll discuss cold-weather gear in the clothing chapter, see page 105). Is it because of overconfidence in the ability to save yourself and get back on your kayak and/or swim for dry land? Some of that happens too, with and without a PFD. People die of exhaustion. Check the United States Coast Guard website and look at the statistics for yourself. It's not pleasant reading, but it is enlightening. People die in boats and kayaks every day. As with any adventure sport, there will always

Even on shallow water pan fishing trips, wear your PFD! Finding a comfortable PFD is the key to wearing it every time you head out.

be tragic accidents, but the brutal truth is that most of these deaths could have been prevented. A great number of the victims would have survived had they been wearing an appropriate PFD.

A personal flotation device is not a magic bullet that will save your life. There's one instance, though, in which it can be your only hope: if you black out due to illness or exhaustion and fall into the water, or (more likely) are knocked unconscious in a mishap that causes you to end up in the water. *You can't swim while you're unconscious. Not today, not ever.* Later on, in the safety section (see page 145), we'll talk about purposefully capsizing your kayak to practice getting back into it. This is a good drill and, on a warm day, can be a lot of fun. Unfortunately, most instances in which your kayak flips aren't going to be controlled and under pleasant circumstances. There probably won't be a sandy beach and tropical water temperature. You're likely to flip in cold current, in an area with multiple water hazards such as submerged rocks and boulders. Bad things typically happen under bad circumstances.

I'm reminded of a good friend's first trip on his stand-up kayak. He managed to get standing upright in short order, but, while he was testing the stability of the deck, the opposite end of the kayak ran up on a submerged branch, and the kayak flipped up on its end at the moment of imbalance. My friend could easily have been conked in the head by the boat, by one of his tackle boxes, or even his paddle as everything rained down around him. As it was, all that was damaged was his pride, and all that was lost was some gear. If it had gone badly, however, and he was knocked unconscious, he could very likely have died face down in that backwater creek and not been found for days—*if he had not been wearing his PFD.* He was wearing his PFD, however, and chances are that if he'd been rendered unconscious, at some point he would have awakened—still floating in the creek—and been able to recover himself and (most of) his gear.

You can't swim if you're unconscious. It's the single biggest reason that PFDs save lives. I could give you many more examples.

However, I tell you these by way of saying that I and one of my closest fishing companions have both endured bad experiences that, handled improperly or without a lot of luck present, very well might have resulted in death. I don't have to search for stories about strangers. It happened to me, and it can happen to you. The single best way of ensuring that you return home to your friends and loved ones at the end of a long day of kayak fishing is to wear your PFD.

Not just *have* one, but *wear* one.

When I finally started getting serious about a PFD for kayak fishing, I picked up a cheap, discount store PFD. It fit me and was rated well for flotation for a person of my size, which was all that mattered to me when I tried it on. It worked fine for canoeing, which I also enjoy, but when it came to kayak fishing and paddling, the armholes were too restrictive and made paddling very unpleasant. I endured a great deal of chafing. Also, with the high seat backs of sit-on-top kayaks, the padding on the back of the cheap PFD would not allow me to sit back, or, worse, it would ride up and push the entire PFD up around my neck. The PFD was also black and heavy. On hot days, it was an exercise in heat exhaustion to wear it for more than an hour-long paddle. It was a nightmare. Can you guess where it ended up? Typically, in the bottom of my kayak or behind the seat. Had I capsized and been rendered unconscious, it would have been found floating near my body, I'm sure. Pretty embarrassing, really.

It wasn't long before I started researching PFDs made specifically for kayaking. Like paddles, PFDs aren't extremely expensive propositions, although there are some high-end PFDs (as with anything else) if you have money to burn. Like paddles, however, they're a necessity. Also like paddles, you'll probably end up buying a cheaper one before you buy a better one. A really good, solid PFD can be had for less than a hundred dollars. Even *much less* than a hundred dollars can get you a great PFD. There are now several dozen PFDs flooding the market that are geared toward kayak fishermen, with extra pockets and gadgets, and we'll talk about them in a bit. For now, what you need is something that will keep you afloat when the stuff hits the fan, or your head hits a sunken boulder.

Before getting into the nuts and bolts of PFD requirements, types, and styles, I'd like to highly recommend once again that you visit the US Coast Guard Website (USCGBoating.org) for updated information. Kayaking in general, and kayak fishing in particular, is increasing in popularity and I wouldn't be at all surprised to see the Coast Guard tightening up on regulations regarding PFDs in the very near future. Rather than give you specific information in this section that may already be outdated, please consult the Coast Guard information as well as the laws that govern your home state or those states to which you may be traveling. Many states also have safety requirements that are stricter than the Coast Guard requirements. It's up to you to know them!

TYPES OF PFDS

The US Coast Guard recognizes several classifications (types) of PFDs. Some of these are not practical for kayak fishing, or kayaking in general, but let's take a very brief overview of all of them. The USCG requires that each type of PFD meet minimum buoyancy requirements—that is, the force required to keep a person's head and chin above the water. More detailed descriptions are available at USCGboating.org.

Type I

Not usually associated with kayaking, a Type I PFD is considered an "offshore life jacket." These are large, bulky, and brightly colored. They also have the most buoyancy and generally have the ability to turn unconscious people face up in the water. These

Check the PFD tag to help determine if it's the right one for you.

PFDs encompass what you knew as the typical, ugly "life jacket" when you were a kid. Type I offers a lot of protection but, due to its bulkiness, isn't well suited to paddling in a small kayak (or even a large one). The minimum required adult buoyancy for a Type I PFD is 22 pounds.

Type II

Type II PFDs are considered "near shore vests." Designed for calmer, inland waters where a relatively fast rescue is likely, they have the ability to turn some (but not all) unconscious wearers face up in the water. They are not as bulky as Type I PFDs and may be suitable for paddling. The minimum required adult buoyancy for Type II PFDs is 15.5 pounds.

Type III

Known as "flotation aids," Type III PFDs are what you'll commonly see most (smart) kayak anglers wearing. They're recommended where there's a chance for a quick rescue (as in most nonremote fishing areas). Type III offer the least restriction of movement, when comparing the first three first types of PFDs. Since the comfort and movement factor is very high, the kayak angler is more likely to keep this vest on all day. The minimum required adult buoyancy for a Type III PFD is 15.5 pounds, just as their bulkier counterparts, the Type II. Keep that in mind.

Type IV

Type IVs are known as "throwable devices." You've seen them. They're typically cushions or rings designed to be thrown to someone in need of rescue. They are not for nonswimmers, rough waters, or (obviously) someone who is unconscious. As of this writing, there is no requirement that these be carried on canoes or kayaks. I have always carried one on my kayaks. Rings and cushions are required to have minimum adult buoyancy of 16.5 and 18.0 pounds. That's a fair amount of buoyancy for something that isn't considered completely practical or necessarily desirable in a lifesaving situation, and that is why I always carry one.

Type V

These are special use devices. We're not going too deeply into Type V for the purposes of this book, because they are required for water sports far beyond the pale of kayaking and kayak fishing.

Inflatable PFDs

Inflatable life vests offer an interesting alternative to other PFDs and are a rapidly developing technology. The Coast Guard is looking into narrowing down these classifications and including the use of inflatables (some of which are now listed as a Type III) and inflatable hybrids. Some are vests, while others can be waist packs. This author's personal opinion on inflatables is that yes, they offer almost unlimited movement; but the big sticking point for me is that manual versions need to have a cord pulled for inflation. Once again, you can't swim when you're unconscious. There are models coming onto the market that inflate when they come into contact with water. How realistic these PFDs will be for a sport as inherently *wet* as kayak fishing remains to be seen. These are developments we all need to keep an eye on, especially when it comes to the hybrid vests. Like many things in the kayak angling world, the technology is developing more rapidly than the regulators and anglers who use and review them have time to disseminate the information.

PFD STYLES

Now that you're well versed in the types of PFDs, what should you get? I'm a firm believer in getting a lightweight, cool PFD as your first purchase. Choose one large enough to fit over bulky clothes or wet/dry suits (more on those later, see page 108) for cold-weather fishing, but small enough for those hot tank top days of mid-August. Size may be a compromise, but getting something in between those two clothing requirements will ensure that you don't have to run out and buy a second vest for cooler or warmer conditions—at least not right away.

Now that you know the type (probably Type III, at least to start), where should you begin to narrow down the best PFD for you? Styles include pull-over, side entry, or (most commonly) zip up the front. I like the zip up the front style, just for ease of taking it on and off. Of particular necessity in kayaking are large arm-holes, a deep neck, and thin shoulder straps. Kayaking PFDs tend to be shorter in length (shoulder to waist) than those designed for

Your PFD should fit over cold-weather clothing.

other water sports. This is to facilitate the high backs often found on fishing kayaks. I prefer a mesh back so there is no interference with the seat back. Most mesh-backed kayak PFDs have a single buoyant panel high enough up on the back so that it doesn't interfere with the seat at all. I also prefer as much mesh on the vest as possible, so you don't overheat during those dog days of summer. If you've properly fitted the vest, you can always add warmer layers underneath for cooler outings, but there isn't a whole lot you can do to alleviate the heat on a hot day. Unfortunately, what happens is that anglers with overly warm PFDs tend to take them off on hot days. For all the reasons stated in this chapter, that's a poor choice. If you're comfortable, you'll keep it on. The same can be said for fit. Try them on until you find one that fits you and *then* find a chair (or better yet a kayak, if there's one available) and see how it fits while you're in the position in which you'll most frequently be wearing it. If it rides up around your neck and chin, keep looking.

As mentioned earlier, there are PFDs now being marketed specifically for kayak fishermen. I'm ambivalent about these. Typically, they have many more pockets than a standard Type III short-waisted kayak PFD and some offer fold-down "platforms" on which to do your rigging. There may also be various lanyards and tool holders. I saw one yesterday with a drink holder in it. Yes, a PFD with a drink holder. These vests purport to be a kind of hybrid between a fishing vest and a PFD, but in my opinion, they aren't necessary. One of the elements of kayak angling I enjoy the most is simplifying. If you've rigged your kayak properly, most of what you need should be within reach of you (and you probably even have a cup holder nearby!). Fishing vests, for those who have owned one (or a dozen) tend to be dumping grounds for bits and pieces of fishing paraphernalia and also end up being just one more thing that has to be organized before a fishing trip. Simple tackle boxes (and trays), as we'll discuss in the rigging chapter of the book (see page 223), can easily hold all your gear in an organized fashion. My thought on the matter is if you have enough gear stashed in your PFD to really make a difference, you may be affecting that streamlined design you so carefully selected and are now adversely affecting your paddling. I may buy a fishing PFD one of these days so I can have a few more places to misplace my tools and tackle, but not today.

WHAT COLOR?

Many kayak anglers go the high-visibility route and select vests that are brightly colored to aid in visibility to other watercraft and to increase the likelihood of water rescue should the angler go into the drink. As with kayak color, I'm of the drab mindset. I like low-key colors for my fishing activities. That said, *every life vest you consider* should have reflective markings on it. This will aid in night visibility to your paddling partners and other boats, as well as increase your visibility to other boaters in broad daylight. The reflective patches tend to be small but are highly effective in both lowlight and daylight conditions.

MATERIALS OF CONSTRUCTION

Material of construction is probably not going to be a high priority for your PFD selection. You'll probably find a PFD that fits you, that looks good to you, and that has glowing reviews on your favorite kayak fishing forum. Material of construction may never enter your mind, but let's briefly talk about it before moving on to the next section. Polyvinyl chloride (PVC) foam is an inexpensive material, durable, and is frequently used in the manufacture of PFDs across the entire spectrum of price and design. Kapok is a material that has the added benefit of being natural. It comes from the seeds of the Kapok tree and is more durable than foam while still being very light and very water resistant. Another material you'll find in some PFDs goes by the trademarked name of Gaia. It is softer than PVC and is chemical- and heat-resistant. As mentioned in several other chapters of the

Proper PFD selection is one of the most important decisions you will make.

book, the technology is evolving and frequently changing. Keep up on the latest materials of construction for PFDs, and you may find something even more suited to your style, comfort level, and budget.

PFD CARE

I always find it humorous to see the warning about storing PFDs in sunlight because the ultraviolet (UV) rays can degrade the materials. The same often holds true for kayaks. Everything's fine. Just don't take it out in the sun . . . In truth, storing your PFD in a shaded area is probably a good idea and will likely give it a bit longer lifespan.

Other care tips for your PFD include avoiding the use of harsh detergents that could degrade the outer materials and possibly adversely affect the foam beneath. Kayak fishing PFDs can get stinky with sweat and fish slime, so you will want to wash yours from time to time. Gentle detergents, water, and a good sponge cleaning will go a long way toward assuring you're not scaring off your fishing partners and local wildlife with the noxious smell of your PFD. Often, a simple rinse in fresh water after fishing is all it takes to keep your PFD up to snuff—or sniff. Always let your PFD dry in the open air before storage to prevent mildew.

Other than cleaning, there are a few things that can help prolong the life of your PFD. For instance, don't put overly heavy items in the pockets, as this can cause stress on seams and premature failure. Common sense should tell you not to add heavy things to the PFD you need to keep you floating should things go bad. Also, try to avoid kneeling or sitting on the PFD (you should be wearing it, anyway!), because this can compromise the integrity of its buoyancy by compressing the foam.

Finally, when disposing of an old PFD that is no longer buoyant or functional, please cut it up into several pieces. There are a surprising number of garbage pickers out there. You don't want to see your unsafe PFD being sold the following weekend at your neighbor's garage sale to some unsuspecting kayak fisherman who is trying to save a few bucks.

Safety first!

Clothing for Kayak Fishing

Your kayak is in your garage, or already strapped to your truck, while you impatiently wait for a day off. You have your paddle, and you've carefully selected a personal flotation device that fits, will save your life, and looks pretty cool, despite the fact you really didn't want to have to wear one. Before we move on to all of the more interesting (and fun!) gear associated with kayak fishing, let's take a quick look at clothing selection. "Come on," you're saying, "enough already! It's eighty degrees today, the water is seventy-two, and I have a baseball cap, a pair of shorts, and T-shirt that will work just fine. I just want to get that thing out on the water and make a cast or two. I'm dyin' here!" I hear you, my friend. I hear you. If it's eighty and the water is seventy, those three items along with your PFD and some footwear are all you need. *Go for it.* Chances are, however, that you're really going to enjoy kayak fishing. (There's a very slim chance that you're *not*.) As you grow into the sport and it gets later in the season, you may find that you're still wanting to fish. Or maybe you find your first few voyages taking place in the early cold water of spring in the northern parts of the country. Learning a few things about kayak clothing selection can (here we go again) save your life. You can thank me later.

BASIC GEAR AND WARM-WEATHER KAYAK FISHING CLOTHING

For basic warm-condition fishing trips, when water temperature is above 60 degrees Fahrenheit and the combined air and water temperature is above 120 degrees (this is a good rule of thumb to remember), you're safe with minimal clothing. At higher temperatures, especially in a sit-on-top kayak where getting wet is a normal part of the day, you'll find the exposure to water to be a welcome relief, especially on those steamy days.

No matter the time of year or temperature, a hat is always recommended. Skin cancer is a serious consideration, and shading your head and face from harmful UV rays is always a wise choice (and should be accompanied by the use of sunscreen). A wide-brimmed fishing hat will shade your head and face from multiple angles. A hat has the added benefit of offering a layer of protection from hooks, screwed up backcasts, and the occasional angry seagull or swallow. More than once my hat has been ripped off by the treble hooks of my lure, and I was happy that it was my hat that went flying into the drink—and not my ear. If you're a flyfisherman, you know how easily a tiny, size-twelve fly can find its way into your earlobe and bury itself all the way up to the barb. There's no mystery in why almost every flyfisherman in the world wears a hat. Wear a hat!

For those warm-weather days, it's tempting to wear only a T-shirt or a tank top, especially in warmer climates. I do a lot of that, myself. But there are also great long-sleeved shirts first popularized in the Florida Keys that are well suited to those hot days and offer a bit more protection than short sleeves. They're usually made of lightweight materials, have vents in the armpits (and possibly the sides and back), and offer another layer of protection against UV rays, insect bites, fish hooks, and whatever vegetation you may find yourself ducking under as you push the limits up that favorite, tiny creek of yours.

Warm weather pants typically consist of the above-mentioned shorts, though I often prefer a very lightweight pair of pants, again, as protection against the sun, bugs, hooks, and whatever else you might encounter during a day on the water. Like fishing shirts, there are many lightweight pants on the market (fishing and otherwise) that will fit this need. During warm weather, I wear a very light pair of long pants that I picked up from a discount store for less than ten bucks. It doesn't have to be anything fancy, and you'll thank yourself when you don't have to come home and spray your thighs down with sunburn relief medication.

I'm going to talk about footwear at the end of this chapter, but I'll mention it briefly here. In the warm weather, you'll see a lot of kayak fishermen in sandals, sneakers, or even barefoot. I've done all of the above. The only time it matters, other than offering protection from all of the above hazards (including any hooks and lures that may be lurking around the deck of your boat), is that you'll want to consider *some kind* of footwear when launching and landing your kayak. Boat launches, creek edges, and beaches are notoriously strewn with discarded fishing gear, broken bottles, and rusty metal; and it's simply too easy to pick up a hook or, worse, a jagged piece of hundred-year-old beer can in the sole of your foot. An injury to the foot can put a quick end to a fishing day, and the infections that often accompany aquatic wounds are not pleasant to deal with. In a pinch, a pair of sandals or an old pair of sneakers will work fine, even if you just slip them on for launching and landing. There are better options, though, that we'll discuss later.

COLD-WEATHER CLOTHING

Most boating deaths—close to 90 percent in any given year—happen in cold water. When the water temperature drops below 60 degrees Fahrenheit, and the combined temperature of the air and water is below 120 degrees, kayak fishermen very seriously need to consider dressing for the temperature. It's not just a matter of putting on a warm hunting coat under your PFD, or a good pair of long johns. If that's all you have, it's adequate for most conditions, but as the water temperature (and chances of surviving taking a swim) dip, there are far better options you should consider.

SPLASH PANTS AND SPLASH JACKETS

When temps are cooling off but still near the range listed above, "splash pants" and "splash jackets" may be effective. These are typically fairly lightweight (sometimes insulated) garments that are waterproof. These will prevent incidental splashing from your paddle or waves. Also, if you're seat-wrestling with a twenty-pound lake trout, it will stop you from getting soaked, causing a dangerous refrigeration effect (especially with low air temperatures and windchills). You can quickly transition from a great day fishing to a point where you're battling hypothermia. If you take a swim, they will take on water and will not save your life if you're in the water for any length of time. For comfort's sake, however, a splash suit can make a normal day on the cool water much more pleasant. There are many manufacturers of splash pants and jackets made specifically for the paddle sports, but you can do as well with a pair of comfortable, waterproof hunting pants and a jacket if you already own (or prefer) them.

WET SUITS

A wet suit, really? Sound a little too far out there for you? Just consider it for a moment. Wet suits are constructed of neoprene, just as are heavy-gauge fishing waders. When water temps are below 60 degrees, the common paddler's wisdom says to "dress for immersion." Most of us would rather not consider being *immersed* in forty-degree water. The cold-shock alone can cause your reactions to slow and your stress level to rise. Immersion in cold water *kills*. When immersed, the layer of neoprene traps a thin layer of water next to your body. Your body heats that water, just as it heats the air in your clothing on dry land, and provides a level of insulation *even in the water*.

Research should be done when selecting a wet suit. The thicker the neoprene, the more difficult movement becomes. If you're trying to get back on your sit-on-top on a cold day in a cold lake, you don't want your movement dangerously restricted. There are many, many options out there for full-body wet suits. Many paddlers' wet suits come with open armholes (tank top style). These obviously allow for better movement and (also obviously) give more places for cold water to penetrate the suit. Read those individual reviews from people who have tried each kind before deciding which one is best for you. If possible, go to a real kayak shop and try on several different styles and types.

Wet suits are typically used as a layer, with a base-layer beneath, wet suit, then outer clothing such as a splash suit. Wet suits tend to be reasonably priced compared to dry suits, which are up next.

DRY SUITS

Dry suits, unlike wet suits, are made to keep you dry, in the water and out. Their thermal properties come from trapping a warm layer of *air* around the body, unlike wet suits, which will keep a layer of water warmed. Wet suits = wet. Dry suits = dry. Wet suits should keep you warm when submerged. Dry suits *should* keep you mostly dry *and* warm. It really is that simple.

Dry suits are constructed from a waterproof fabric. The dry suit can be a part of a good layering system, but they typically *are* the outer layer. They don't provide warmth. That is the job of a good base layer (good thermal underwear), as well as a middle layer, such as fleece. Dry suits often employ wrist, ankle, and neck gaskets to keep water from permeating the suit, keeping it away from your body. These gaskets are very tight and, incidentally, are often the reason many anglers choose wet suits. Also, for anglers with a big head (like me—it's huge!), the ability to squeeze one's head through the neck opening needs to be checked. Not everyone can do it. The gaskets are commonly constructed of latex, as well. Latex allergies may rule out the use of a particular dry suit. Check materials of construction and (as always) as many user reviews as is possible before buying your dry suit. Dry suits, other than the gasket issue, are generally thought to be more comfortable than wet suits once donned.

Dry suits can be considerably more expensive than wet suits. Often a good dry suit will run four or five times more than a good wet suit. As always, your budget is something that needs to be considered. A decent, well-priced wet suit is far better protection than a dry suit that you're saving up for but don't yet have in your possession.

PUTTING IT ALL TOGETHER

Many cold-water kayak anglers use a combination of the items listed above. Depending on the weather, most anglers fishing in temps cold enough to warrant a wet suit will be layered in thermal undergarments, fleece, and an outer splash jacket and/or splash pants. The splash jacket may also be what's referred to as a "dry top" by some paddlers. It's the same basic idea: a waterproof outer garment. PFD goes on the outside, as always. A good winter hat that provides warmth and wind resistance is also a must.

Kayak fishermen in a dry suit will likely utilize a base layer and a mid layer. The dry suit can function as the outer layer, though an additional layer such as a splash jacket will likely be employed.

Author with cool-weather gear (splash pants and splash jacket, neoprene wading shoes) paddling comfortably on a windy, forty-degree day. Polarized glasses and hat add to the safety and protection factor.

The ability to add and subtract layers is a logical consideration. There are many days when the air temperature starts out at subfreezing but turns into a balmy forty or fifty degrees by the late morning or early afternoon. At fifty degrees, a kayak angler may be suffering in a wet or dry suit and too many layers. The ability to peel off a few layers for comfort is an important consideration.

GLOVES

We're not going too deeply into gloves for kayak fishing. There are a host of paddling gloves and ten million and one waterproof gloves or neoprene gloves made for fishing. I find that in cold weather, gloves for paddling are a very important consideration. Paddles get cold, even the spiffy, expensive carbon fiber paddles, though they get less cold than the aluminum paddles. For fishing, I've tried them all. Neoprene, waterproof wool, some of the fancy new thin synthetics that purport to offer unlimited dexterity, and many others I can't recall. Frankly, even in the coldest temperatures (whether kayak fishing, fly fishing, or ice fishing), I usually go bare-handed while handling rods, reels, lines, and lures. It's impossible, with any type of glove, to enjoy the dexterity needed for many situations on the water. I don't, however, risk frostbite. How? I generally keep a pair of good, insulated rag-wool gloves nearby in which to slip my hands as soon as the rigging, landing, tying, or fish releasing is done. Many spinning and baitcasting reels can be cast with a decent pair of gloves, but I've never met a single knot I could tie while wearing them. Another gadget I've employed extensively for cold-weather fishing (and hunting) is what an old-timer might call a "muff." It's simply a tube in which to slip your hands. Place a few chemical hand-warmers in it, and it becomes an oasis of heat on a frigid day. Whether employing gloves or a muff, keeping a dry towel nearby to wipe off fish slime or water from your hands before slipping them into dry warmth will go a long way toward keeping your hands warm for the long haul on a cold day of kayak angling.

KAYAK ANGLING FOOTWEAR

As mentioned in the introduction to this section, the choices about what you put on your feet when kayak angling can be simple. It depends, of course. Is it warm and sunny? You're probably tempted to go barefooted. I've done it many times. Flip-flops and sandals, however, offer at least a small layer of protection for your feet against hooks and submerged objects when launching and landing. Are you fishing in saltwater where there is a real threat of stinging organisms that may pierce the soles of your feet and make for a day of misery? Are you a sloppy kayak keeper? Is the deck of your 'yak littered with bait hooks and treble hooks and in-line hooks? You get the point. (Hopefully, you don't get the point). If so, don't go barefoot! Wear something, even if it's just an old pair of sneakers that double as your lawnmowing footwear.

There are many waterproof shoes on the market as well as items that would be more correctly described as socks. Neoprene socks are a good option to slip on and off for launching and landing if you prefer to go barefoot. Many are now reinforced so they blur the line between sock and shoe. They also complement wet suits and dry suits very well and can often be combined with warmer inner layers such as insulated socks. Wading shoes, particularly those designed for saltwater anglers, are a great warm-water alternative to heavy neoprene. Many kayak anglers like to jump out of their kayaks and wade at various times, either to fish or to drag their kayak through shallow runs. Foot protection is crucial during these times, and there are many types of footwear that can fit the bill for kayaking and wading. The choices for paddling footwear are almost endless. You need to select footwear that matches the temperatures in which you're fishing, the conditions you are likely to encounter, and the level of protection from the elements that you are seeking.

HATS

Whether the weather is warm or whether it is not (trying saying that fast five times!), you need a hat. As mentioned above, a hat in warm weather (preferably one with a bit of a brim) offers protection from sunburn and errant fishing lures, not to mention those unexpected branches and thorns under which you thought you had plenty of clearance. Hats and fishing go together. The sillier they look, the fewer people will bother you and ask questions about your favorite fishing hole.

During cold weather, a warm hat—preferably a wool blend—that has some waterproof and wind-resistant qualities is an absolute requirement. Cold days are one thing, but cold days on the water tend to amplify that feeling of gnawing coldness that seeps right down to the base of your very being. A hat that keeps your head warm will go a long way to ward keeping the rest of your body warm. Find the best cold-weather knit hat you can afford. It will pay for itself many times over during a cold day on the water.

POLARIZED FISHING GLASSES

I've been wearing polarized glasses almost since they first came out. They're invaluable for sight fishing. They're also invaluable for seeing what it is that you're fighting at the other end of the line. The uses and value of a decent pair (or even a cheap pair!) of polarized glasses for a fisherman can't be overstated.

For a *kayak* angler, however, the polarized glasses that you may or may not typically use for fishing are a very important addition in the safety kit of any conscientious individual. Kayak fishing can be on wide open water or it can be in timber-choked backwater creeks. The ability to spot underwater hazards increases greatly with the use of polarized glasses. Next to your PFD, they are one of the single most important pieces of safety gear, in my opinion. They're not only useful on small, woodsy water, either. The ability to rig gear in the glare of midday, spot schools of fish, see rising fish or (perish the thought) an approaching powerboat makes the glasses worth their weight in molded plastic, if not gold.

Glasses-keepers or lanyards are a must, unless you're interested in swimming to retrieve them. Been there, done that.

Transporting Your Kayak

Okay, *now* you're ready to go. Right? A couple of chapters ago, your kayak was tied to your truck, straps checked, but then you got waylaid by this talk of expensive paddles, clothing, and the all-important PFD. You grew frustrated with your intrepid author and thought, "Damn, why didn't I think of that?" At least I hope that's happened a few times in the last several dozen pages. And then it was back to the Internet forums, the kayak shop, and possibly somewhere between one and fifteen more online orders that finally arrived and added to your growing pile of what you've described to your spouse as *necessities*. Your kayak has been on and off the roof rack a half-dozen times while you go about the business of your day job, double-checking your checking account balance to make sure that you have enough left for gas money to get down to the lake. But—and you're going to hate me for this—before you go, let's talk *about going*. Transporting your kayak, unless you're fortunate enough to live on the water and have a dock in your yard, is something that you're going to have to do each and every time you want to go fishing. It can be simple and painless with just a few precautions and a good plan. Let's spend a few minutes considering your options.

CARGO BARS AND RACKS

Many SUVs these days come standard with some kind of rooftop cargo rack with crossbar setup. These can certainly do the job of safely hauling your fishing rig with a bit of ingenuity and some careful planning. The kayak will typically ride upside down or completely right-side up. For cars and other vehicles without cargo racks and crossbars, inexpensive cargo bars can be purchased that strap to the car, usually into the window slots. A permanent or temporary set of cargo bars can be an economical solution for getting your fishing kayak to the water. At some point, however, you're going to want to purchase a set of kayak racks to add further security to your fishing travels and to protect your kayak gear, especially if you plan on doing any amount of long- or medium-distance travel to your fishing destination. Racks are usually universal and can be attached to most factory and aftermarket crossbars. Let's look at racks and see what's out there.

KAYAK ROOF RACKS

Roof racks are by far the most common way that kayak anglers transport their boats. From the very basics, such as using a few pool noodles or foam cradles and strapping the boat down, to cargo racks fitting with J-racks or V-racks. Other rooftop accessories that aid in overhead handling of heavy kayaks are variations on rollers that fasten to the back of the vehicle and help prevent damage to its paint job, and to your kayak. J-racks are most common for rooftop carry. They're simple and effective, and they hold the kayak in a slanted position, while offering ease of access for loading the boat from the side or back of the vehicle. J-racks can be attached by a host of methods but typically are mounted to the cargo rack of most SUVs or other improvised bars on your kayak-hauling vehicle. J-racks come in many sizes and varieties. Some fold down and out of the way when they're not needed. They can vary widely in size, and kayak fishermen (especially those with heavy, wide boats) often go for the larger models. A good set of racks may cost anywhere from one hundred to three hundred dollars. That said, I got by just fine with some cheap, small J-racks I found on Amazon for around forty dollars a set. Higher-quality racks typically offer better materials of construction, better welds, and better construction in general. Also, the bargain-basement racks (such as my first sets) tend to have foam coatings that fail or wear out quickly. I fixed mine with electrical tape, and they're still going strong. More expensive racks will have thicker, more durable foam padding and a sturdier mounting base.

V-racks are another excellent option for cartopping your kayak. As with J-racks, there are many variations, styles, and sizes, but they almost all consist of a two-piece construction with mounting bases that attach directly to your cargo rack and/or cargo bar. Composed of two pieces, the racks can be positioned at any distance apart you desire. This allows the V-rack to be set at the exact width that your kayak requires for secure transport. A snug fit to start with ensures a more secure ride, especially once the kayak is strapped down (more on that later). V-racks generally require that the kayak either be carried upside down, or right-side up, though I've seen some V-racks configured to carry fishing kayaks at a slight angle. With sit-on-top kayaks, transporting upright doesn't cause an issue because, with their scupper holes, they are not going to fill with rain should you happen to drive through a monsoon. Laugh if you want, but a kayak filled with water presents serious danger both to vehicle stability on the road and the person who has to try to get it down. Most sit-inside kayaks are transported upside down, just for this reason. A few inches of water can mean hundreds of extra pounds and possible damage to your car, your kayak, and you.

Kayak cradles are becoming increasingly popular in kayak and kayak-fishing circles. These cradles represent a completely different design than more traditional racks but function very much like a low-profile V-rack. The streamlined profile has a V-notch, providing a greater surface area resulting in added friction for excellent stability. There are many designs on the market right now, and many more coming out all the time.

The kayak rack market is exploding, like many other aspects of the kayak-fishing industry. Do your homework, read the reviews, and compare your kayak specs and measurements to the measurements and specifications listed for the rack you're interested in.

OTHER MODES OF TRANSPORT

One of my favorite ways to carry my angling kayaks has been to slide them into the back of my pickup truck, utilizing a fantastic piece of gear known as a tailgate extender. The L-shaped piece of steel slides into the receiver hitch and effectively extends the truck bed an additional several feet. This is ideal for short-trip kayak hauling. Throw it in the truck, strap it down, drive to your spot, and simply slide it off and into the water. It allows for carrying the kayak upright, and as fully rigged as you feel like carrying. It's fast, effective, and great for brief trips. With the kayak (especially larger boats) sticking out past the tailgate, though supported by the extender, make sure you use adequate flagging on the bow (or stern) and also verify that you're adhering to your state and local laws dealing with loads extending past the gate. This quick and dirty alternative is a great option for the kayak angler with a pickup truck.

Speaking of pickup trucks, there are several racks on the market now that attach to the stake holes and allow for easy overhead carry of one or more kayaks. These racks closely resemble commercial ladder racks seen on construction trucks. Those ladder racks, incidentally, also serve many kayak fishermen well as an alternative to the kayak-specific racks.

Kayak Trailers

My evolution through kayak transportation happened quickly. With an SUV and a pickup truck at my disposal, I cartopped with and without racks and carried the kayak in the back of my truck with and without a tailgate extender. When the time came to get rid of my notoriously undependable pickup, and with a growing collection of kayaks on my hands (one of which is comparatively heavy), I elected to purchase a trailer for my kayak hauling, at least over longer distances and with my heavier boat. I figured,

A trailer is an excellent option for heavy kayaks, and it allows the kayak to remain rigged and ready to go.

correctly, that a trailer would allow me to keep the boat rigged with all but the most fragile equipment, keep it upright, and provide a much more ergonomic platform from which to launch the boat, in almost every circumstance. With a trailer, I'd never again have to hoist my boats over my head.

Initially, I planned to buy an inexpensive utility trailer and modify it with crossbars and tie-down eyes. The general design of most bargain-basement utility trailers, however, consists of a short tongue and small wheels that aren't rated for realistic highway speeds. The bigger, longer trailers with bigger wheels and better speed ratings tended to be heavy and more expensive. At the outset, I ignored the trailers on the market designed specifically to haul kayaks and canoes. They seemed overpriced, and I wasn't going to pay too much money if I could modify a cheaper trailer in a weekend DIY project. However, when I started adding up what an *adequate* utility trailer would cost, along with the additional hardware, crossbars, and other modifications I'd certainly want to add, I turned my attention back to the over-the-counter kayak trailers.

Commercial kayak trailers (like kayaks, paddles, and PFDs) come in a wide array of designs, materials of construction, and, of course, price. The features they all have in common include a small, lightweight frame, a long tongue, crossbars (sometimes with racks already installed, for a fee), and tie-down points for straps and ropes. Most generally come with high-speed wheels, as well.

I chose a trailer that was in the neighborhood of nine hundred dollars. It wasn't a heavily rigged trailer, and it required construction (five hours, one Sunday afternoon with my wife and me steadily working and swearing together). It came with all the basics: waterproof lights and wiring harnesses, high-speed wheels, multiple tie-down points, and two square crossbars on which I'd mount either a set of V-racks, J-racks, or both. (I eventually settled on two sets of V-racks, after many different combinations, though that's still subject to change.) After Sunday construction and Monday

Trailers can be configured for multiple kayaks, utilizing any type or combination of rack(s) you prefer.

registration, I hauled my kayak down to the lake on the trailer and haven't looked back since.

Kayak trailers are an awesome way to get your kayak to the fishing hole. With your angling kayak strapped to a trailer, it will generally be less than three feet off the ground. Anyone who has horsed their kayak high overhead—as I have a million times—will tell you that balancing and loading even the most svelte, empty kayak over your head is sometimes an exercise in frustration. I've lost my grip and dropped my kayak down on earth and pavement more times than I care to admit—and probably more times than I can remember. A kayak trailer eliminates the overhead hazard and potential back strains completely. Many anglers who have seen my setup like it but say they wouldn't want to be dependent on a ramp for launching their 'yak. Hogwash. I'm no more dependent on a ramp than they are. Sure, if there's a handy ramp that isn't entertaining a frustratingly long line, I may back the trailer down to the water and slide the boat in. However, like cartopping, the trailer is every bit as adept while pulling over to the side by a creek, lake, or pond and dumping the boat off where it can either be dragged, carried, or carted (see below) down to the water like anyone else. Is turning the trailer around a problem? It hasn't been for me. Even on the tightest roads, the trailer is so light that it can simply be unhooked and spun around in the opposite direction if you're not comfortable backing it up.

Speaking of moving the kayak trailer by hand, this is another part of the setup that I can't say enough about. My entire kayak rig (or rigs, when I'm hauling my wife's or a friend's kayak) can be unhooked from the truck and slid into the garage using one hand. It's almost effortless. I considered adding a folding front wheel, as you see on heavier boat trailers, but soon found that there's absolutely no need. The entire trailer rig, with boats, can easily be moved with one hand, if not just a couple of fingers. If you have garage storage space, the trailer gives you a convenient place to work during your endless hours of kayak rigging and daydreaming. If you don't have garage or outbuilding space, the trailer can conveniently be rolled around behind your house or garage, out of sight and covered with a tarp or kayak cover to keep everything clean. Also, when returning home from kayak angling, the trailer offers a convenient place to hose your boats down. If flipping the boat to drain water while cleaning becomes a necessity, it can rest on the racks or bars, eliminating the need for bending down to work on it on the ground.

Can you tell yet that I love my kayak trailer?

The tradeoff? Kayak trailers are not as simple as an overhead rack setup. Some people don't like hauling trailers, having heard of (or perhaps witnessed) towing nightmares. There is added cost in a trailer, as well as the registration paperwork, likely requiring an aggravating trip to the DMV. Making sure lights are in good working order, tires are properly inflated, and bearings are greased

"Bearing Buddy" and similar devices can eliminate the road hazard of overheated bearings.

before a long trip are all additional things you have to think about if you're considering a kayak trailer. Incidentally, on my last couple of trailers I've installed Bearing Buddies, and I have never had an issue with a bearing overheating on even a long trip, as long as they're filled with grease before heading out. There are tricks to simplify life with a tow-behind trailer, and once you become familiar with them, you'll love your trailer, too.

LOADING YOUR FISHING KAYAK

We're not going to belabor the specifics of getting your kayak onto your car or truck. There are so many types of cars, racks, trailers, and trucks that we couldn't begin to cover everything in a few short pages. Also, the size and weight of your kayak, as well as your own personal height, build, and fitness level come into play.

Fishing kayaks, even the light ones, tend to be big and relatively heavy. Getting them onto cartop racks can be a challenge. Obviously, two people can make this much easier, but very often we find ourselves solo kayak angling. Practice getting your kayak on and off your roof, truck, or trailer at home several times before trying it waterside, when conditions will likely be less than ideal. Sloped ground and wet boat ramps (as well as wet hulls!) make what seemed easy at home a bit more difficult. Add to that the arm and back fatigue that may arise from a day of kayak angling, and it's not going to be as easy as it was in the yard back home.

A good tactic for solo anglers, whether it's putting the boat on a cartop rack or a trailer, is to lift one end onto the rear rack and slide the boat forward until it engages the front rack. With this method, you aren't lifting the entire weight of the kayak at any one time, and you have the added benefit of leverage. This method can be aided by hardware such as rollers that mount to the rear of your vehicle and are made for this purpose. There are also commercial lift systems available from some of the better manufacturers. These vary in size and construction but all are relatively costly. If you find it simply too difficult to manhandle the kayak to comfortably get it on the racks yourself, consider exploring one of these options. Remember, the easier it is for you to load your boat, the more you'll do it, the more you will enjoy it, and the better you'll get at kayak angling. Solo loading can also be accomplished by lifting the boat on from the side of the vehicle and gently lowering it onto the racks. If the car isn't too tall (or you aren't too short!), this is probably the quickest and most controlled method. However, make certain that you're comfortable with the weight of the kayak before attempting it. Good form, such as lifting with your arms and legs instead of your back, is necessary to prevent strains and other injuries. There's a point—as you're lifting the kayak from the ground and trying to turn it over (or angling it)—when most strains and injuries occur.

Practice, practice, practice, and if you never get comfortable with lifting your boat, consider one of the commercial lifting aids that are available, or even a simple set of suction-cup-mounted rollers.

SECURING YOUR KAYAK FOR TRANSPORT

This past year on the way back from a successful Adirondack kayak-angling trip, my wife and I witnessed a car coming down the opposite side of the New York State Thruway. The green kayak on its roof was sideways and looked about ready to come loose. It was easy to see that little thought had gone into the two straps holding it to the roof, one of which had disengaged, leaving the boat hanging on in the seventy-mile-per-hour wind quite literally by a thread. This sight is all too common with cartop kayaks and canoes. I'm quite sure that, at some point shortly after we saw it, that kayak flew off the roof of the little sedan. Maybe it flew off into a ditch or safely into the median and all that was lost was a kayak. Or maybe it cartwheeled off the back of the car and shattered their rear window. Perhaps after that, it flew through the front window of the vacationing family behind them and caused an accident at best or, at worst, killed someone. The price of not securing your kayak, whether it's in a truck bed, cartop, or on a trailer, can be a steep one for everyone involved, including innocent bystanders.

I guess I'm saying that you need to pay attention to this part.

The typical rigging components for loading kayaks are cambuckle straps, ratchet straps, and rope. For our purposes, let's dismiss ropes right away. Some will argue. I'm okay with that. Unless you're an Eagle Scout with several knot badges on your vest, and you have a good stock of seasoned, nonstretch rope, let's avoid using rope. You have extra rope lying around, you say? Fine, use it for anchor lines (coming up), emergency tow-ropes, and shallow water drag ropes for your kayak. Don't skimp and use rope for securing your kayak for road travel. The strapping options available at ridiculously affordable prices make the use of rope for securing your kayak not worth the effort. Very good kayak tie-down options can be found in your local or big-box hardware store for about the same price as a fishing lure.

Cam-buckle straps are typically a simple, spring-loaded strap. The ends are usually J-hooks. The cam-buckles are cinched tight with muscle power and released with the press of a button. They're effective enough for most purposes. Ratchet straps are a bit more complex but very similar in design to cam-buckles. The ratchet straps employ a simple ratchet system that uses mechanical leverage to tighten the straps. Like cam-buckle straps, the ratchet straps are usually tipped with J-hooks. Some kayak enthusiasts insist that the ratchet straps have too much potential for overtightening and cause damage to kayak hulls. I went by that philosophy for some

Cartopping with J-racks, showing proper bow, stern, and belly strapping.

time, until I realized that the kayaks were always more secure over longer distances when using ratchet straps than with cam-buckle straps. Even with cam-buckles, plastic hulls will compress a bit under the tightening of the straps. Ratchet straps offer a tighter strapping job, but, with care taken not to overtighten, you can safely strap down your valuable kayak without damage to the hull. On hot days and long trips, I simply loosen the straps as soon as I arrive at my destination. After hundreds of miles of travel, I've never had a warped or damaged hull. Despite the type of strap used, all straps should be checked periodically for loosening. You'll find that ratchet straps will rarely loosen. The same cannot be said for cam-buckle straps. As you'll see, though, the cam-buckles do have their place.

We'll assume the same rigs in this section for overhead carry or for trailer carry, since they both generally consist of crossbars and racks. Basic rigging for kayak transport begins with strapping the body of the kayak down. Before strapping down, ensure that the kayak is balanced fore and aft and not tipping to one end or the other. The same principles apply whether carrying the kayak angled on its side, upside down, or right-side up. For most angling kayaks, two straps across the belly of the kayak where it rests upon the rack will suffice. Some kayak enthusiasts use three but soon find out the diminishing returns of trying to tighten three straps. They often work against one another, and two of the three straps end up far too tight, risking the hull damage listed above. Two will suffice. The straps should cross the boat very near where the racks engage the kayak. This ensures a secure fit to the rack. Some anglers like to connect the strap directly to the racks. Others prefer to hook the strap to the crossbars. Either way will work. Experiment with both. Remember, the wind resistance and lift on your kayak when traveling at high speeds will be tremendous. If you don't have great faith in the rack mounting system (if you can never seem to get the racks completely tight to the crossbars), you can gain some piece of mind by running the ratchet straps to the crossbar. This prevents the kayak *and* the racks from lifting off your vehicle. Rack failure is more likely than crossbar failure, so this can be a very good option. I prefer to use ratchet straps, as mentioned above, for the belly straps. Don't overtighten. Don't undertighten, either.

Rear view of two angling kayaks on J-racks.

With the two belly straps in place, it's time for the bow and stern lines. This is the sin I see committed most by car-top canoe and kayak travelers. *Bow and stern lines are imperative.* Don't skip these straps, even on short, close-to-home water trips. I see it all the time, and it's just asking for disaster. A strap from the bow down to your front bumper, and from the stern down to your rear bumper, is a safety necessity. These lines are the PFD of your kayak transport. The bow line prevents the kayak from sliding rearward in the event of belly strap failures. The stern line prevents the kayak from sliding forward down over your windshield (or even farther) in the event of a sudden stop or, God forbid, an accident. It's here that most people skimp because there often isn't a simple way to attach the straps on modern vehicles with their plastic bumpers. Pop your hood, though, and you'll see many places near the top of your radiator that will accept your J-hook and still allow the hood to close. The thin, webbed straps run easily between the hood and the radiator frame. In the rear, there's often a trailer hitch available for tie-off, or look up under the rear bumper for a bumper mounting bracket. There's always something to which you can attach the lines. Don't skip this step! For further simplification, this is where I prefer cam-buckles. They don't have to be overly tight—or at least not as tight as the belly lines—and the cam-buckle arrangement is simple to tighten and loosen when loading and unloading. Many kayak transporters prefer two bow lines and two stern lines for further stabilization. There's nothing wrong with that, and it does give an added layer of stability. I haven't found a huge difference between double or single bow and stern lines. My basic rig is two ratchet straps for the belly, and a cam-buckle strap for bow and stern lines. I use this setup whether trailering or car-topping and haven't had a failure yet.

For any length trip, I usually drive a few miles and check and tighten *all* of my straps before continuing on. For longer trips, I check the straps at least once every hour or two. It's a good excuse to get out and stretch your legs and further insurance against a

Cartopping on a full-sized pickup truck.

catastrophic loss. Keep in mind that, while traveling, the kayak adds a fair amount of wind resistance that will be more noticeable in a stiff cross-breeze. Steering may be slightly affected by the altered aerodynamics of a car or truck carrying a kayak or two. On days with a stiff cross-breeze, check your rigging more frequently. Another safety tip worth mentioning is that anything loose in your kayak should either be removed or carried in your car or very solidly secured in your kayak. Anything in the kayak is going to be buffeted by hurricane-force winds, and they will vacuum out anything from a loose spinnerbait to your very expensive PFD. Maybe you'll just lose them, or maybe your favorite Rapala will be wrapped around the antenna of the very angry driver behind you. When in doubt, either secure your gear in a closed hatch or (better yet) in your vehicle.

Cross-Country Transport—Carts and Dollies

So you finally got down to the water for your maiden voyage. You lifted your kayak off the roof or the trailer using proper, ergonomic techniques. You hadn't quite gotten to the rigging and fishing chapters of this book yet, but you had your paddle, PFD, and some fishing gear—and you simply couldn't wait anymore. I don't blame you. But a funny thing may have happened between the parking spot and the water. Maybe you discovered that the parking spot is a *very long way* from the water and that carrying your kayak that far tested the limits of your endurance. By the time you got out on the water and paddled around a bit and practiced flipping your kayak a time or two (next chapter spoiler alert!), you were tired. And maybe, with arms not accustomed to paddling a kayak, you didn't have a whole lot of muscle left to carry your kayak (and all that gear) back to the vehicle, much less hoist it onto the roof. Maybe you're already rethinking this whole "kayak fishing" thing and thinking it's for the birds. *Why didn't I just fork over the tens of thousands of dollars for a bass boat and be done with it?*

Hold on, hold on. Chin up.

Kayaks can be heavy. Even a lightweight Brand-X Super Fish Racer may weigh in at seventy-five pounds without fishing gear, electronics, a paddle, bait, or anything else you might see fit to bring along. If you can back down a ramp, or pull conveniently close to the water you want to fish, carrying your kayak and then making multiple trips with your gear might not seem like a chore. I can almost guarantee that at some point in your first few months of kayak angling you're going to find yourself wanting to fish a place without easy access. At the very least you may wind up in a place where you need to ferry your kayak around a deadfall, or up

Planning ahead for transporting your kayak will get you to the fish more quickly!

a trail, or any combination of these things. Kayaks are small and portable, and one of the joys of kayak angling is being able to fish small, hidden backwater areas and small ponds that are simply not accessible to larger boats.

It's time to consider a kayak cart or dolly. You'll thank me later. Maybe sooner than later! We'll refer to them in this chapter as kayak carts because the term cart and dolly are interchangeable when it comes to small two-wheeled carts that are designed to bridge the distance between your parking spot and your fishing hole. As with everything kayak-related, there are several designs on the market. They range from forty dollars to a couple hundred dollars. There are also more DIY plans on the Internet to build a kayak cart than you can count. I almost built one but realized that for the price of tires, PVC pipe, an axle, and a strap or two, I might

A cart or dolly can lighten your load if it's a long distance from the parking area to the water.

as well just buy one. I went cheap and bought a forty-dollar one. Does that sound familiar? It works great for both my SOT and SIK fishing kayaks.

Construction materials are typically either aluminum, steel, or PVC piping for the cradle and supports. The designs are all basically the same, with the exception of the scupper-hole kayak carts that we'll discuss later in this chapter. The piping or tubing creates a cradle upon which the kayak rests, either balanced in the middle, or slightly counterbalanced to the rear. There is generally a single axle and a pair of tires. The tires may be inflatable "all-terrain" tires or small, hard wheels like you'd typically find on an old wheelbarrow. The inflatable tires make an easier drag along uneven ground, while the hard tires work suitably well for concrete, asphalt, and grass. I'd recommend inflatable tires for general purposes, just because they have more flexibility for whatever type of terrain you might encounter. Most carts come with a strap or two to secure the kayak to the cart. You'll need it, especially on uneven terrain.

The other type of kayak cart is the scupper-hole cart. Basically the same as the kayak cart listed above both in design and construction, the scupper-hole cart also employs two upright posts that are designed to run upward through the scupper holes of an SOT kayak, securing it in place. Sounds ingenious, right? It is a pretty nifty design. The problem most often written about is that (especially on cheaper kayaks) the seam sometimes found in the scupper hole where the upper and lower half of the kayak meets can be one of the most damage-prone areas of the kayak. If the kayak is not rotomolded, then putting a scupper-hole cart post up through the holes and horsing it along uneven terrain is inviting unnecessary risk of damage. There's a lot of stress at the point where the posts meet the scupper hole, and, especially with a loaded kayak, that is a lot of weight and torque that the scupper hole is expected to support. Some anglers love their scupper-hole carts. Some have written horror stories on web forums about cracking their new kayaks.

A scupper-hole cart utilizes uprights that run through scupper holes to secure the kayak.

Read the reviews and weigh the ramifications before making your decision.

Whichever type of cart you end up with, there's more to enjoy than simply lightening your burden when parking isn't convenient to your fishing spot. The kayak cart allows you (even in short traverses) to load up all your gear at your vehicle, right into the kayak, and wheel it down to the water's edge. If you even have mild gear-hound tendencies, you'll be making trip after trip from your car to the kayak as you get ready to go. I don't know about you, but when I arrive at the water to fish, I want to get fishing as soon as possible. Multiple trips from the vehicle down to the kayak by the water tend to make me grumpy when I have the fishing itch. With a cart, those trips can be eliminated, as most of your gear can be loaded onto the kayak after it's on the cart, and everything can be taken to the water at once. If you don't want to, you don't even have to return to the car with the cart. Just strap it to the kayak and shove off!

Speaking of having your kayak cart strapped to your kayak, you'll often see river and stream fishermen doing just that. On unfamiliar water, or even on waterways on which you're familiar with barriers, dams, and beaver haunts, the kayak cart can make short work of portaging around obstacles that otherwise might require multiple trips.

Many anglers carry their carts onboard for convenience and possible portages.

One of my home streams became impassable by a giant fallen willow, wedged between two steep banks. Portaging around it was out of the question. Knowing that the pike should be spawning farther north in the small tributary, I didn't want to give up my afternoon. With the cart in my truck, I simply drove a half-mile down the river, carted everything through the woods and down to the water on the opposite side of the strainer, and I was back in business. With the cart strapped to the kayak, if I encountered any other obstacles, I knew that I could make it around them, as well.

As mentioned earlier, there are all kinds of commercial carts and DIY projects. Make sure that the cart fits your kayak and, if it only comes with a cheesy strap, invest a few dollars in a good ratchet strap. A kayak that is wandering all over the cart on a steep trail can turn a simple trip into the sleighride from hell. Ensure a good kayak-to-cart fit, secure it with a strap or two, load up, and get down to the water as quickly as you can. If carrying the cart on the kayak, make sure it is secured in the event of capsizing, as you do with all your gear.

You do secure all your gear, right? If not, we'll chat about that soon enough.

Kayak Storage and Maintenance

STORAGE

How you store your angling kayak will depend on your circumstances and your preferences. There are many commercial hangers on the market designed to hold kayaks on their side and take up little space in the garage, shed, or basement where they may be kept. There is also a plethora of DIY storage methods. Owners of multiple kayaks often build a rack from two-by-four lumber that can accommodate all of their boats. I used to have overhead racks made simply of two pieces of rope, reinforced with two-inch pipes, to hang my kayaks from my garage ceiling rafters. I think the most important consideration for storage is that the kayak be held securely in such a way that doesn't warp the boat and is protected from the elements.

Can you store your kayak outside on a couple of sawhorses and cover it with a tarp? Sure, you can do that. However, by the

Kayak storage is an important consideration.

time you've sunk several hundred or several thousand dollars into your fishing rig, you may want to offer it protection not only from the elements, but from thieves, as well. I currently store my main fishing 'yak on my trailer, where it's rigged and ready to go, in my garage. It's a pain to move my lawnmower and my leaf blower when I need to access them, but I'm willing to make that sacrifice to make sure my favorite toy is properly protected from damage. The other two kayaks are stored overhead with the rope and PVC pipe setup I mentioned. All are secure from thievery and the damaging effects of the sun.

When taking your kayak from storage after a long break (really, you took a break?), check for rodent nests, snakes, spiders, scorpions, and other nasty hitchhikers that you don't necessarily want crawling up your leg while you're bobbing in thirty feet of water.

Kayak trailers allow for easy storage, space permitting.

MAINTENANCE

Speaking of the damaging effects of the sun, there are many marine protectants designed to create a UV barrier to reduce damage to your kayak's hull. Yes, you read that right: sunscreen for your angling kayak! It's well worth the few dollars to protect your investment. It seems silly to talk about storing your kayak where it won't be damaged by the sun, knowing full well most of your fishing time will see your kayak subjected to direct sunlight as well as reflected sunlight. By using the protectant, which is applied very much like car wax, you can prevent damage from occurring while fishing, as well.

Scratches and gouges are the scourge of first-time kayak anglers. Let's just get this out of the way now. You *are* going to scratch your kayak. Whether it is a surprise boulder you run up on, or simply scraping along the base of a concrete launch ramp, your kayak is going to suffer some damage. Obviously, launching in deeper water and avoiding obstacles, in a perfect world, will help reduce the chances of unsightly gouges frequently found on the bow and stern areas of most fishing kayaks, but despite how careful you may be, you're still going to get some damage.

Some kayak angling enthusiasts recommend sanding the deeper gouges. I don't. The damage is already there. Your hull is stronger and thicker than you think. Why add to the damage by removing more material? Where do you stop? I think it's a bad idea. Sandpaper isn't going to make any damage go away, even if it makes it look a bit better.

Depending on your kayak's material of construction, many manufacturers offer repair kits, often consisting of two-part marine epoxy-type materials. These can fix larger gouges that may, in time, become leaks. Whatever approach you select, do your research! Make very, very sure that the repair material you choose is compatible with your kayak hull and comes recommended by the manufacturer. Anything containing solvent has the risk of dissolving your kayak's hull if applied to an incompatible material. Research is your friend. Access your kayak manufacturer's website and look up repair suggestions. Better yet, call their customer-care number and ask for someone who knows about kayak repairs to your specific make and model.

Finally, always check your hardware before heading out on the water. Try to make a habit of doing this each and every time you head out, preferably the night before. Check fish-finder mounts, camera mounts, seat hardware (a very important one!), rod-holders, and electronics. Ensure that, if you have a battery, it's fully charged. Check to ensure that camera batteries are fresh and that you didn't forget your memory cards (did I mention my forty-five-inch pike that never got photographed??). Check that carry straps are tight and that any other equipment that is screwed, bolted, glued, or tied down is also secure. The whole rundown, with a little practice, will take you less than five minutes. It beats the alternative of getting out on the water, a mile from shore, and realizing that the bolt holding your seat back up has disappeared.

In time, you'll find that this preparation, just like checking your rods and tackle, is an enjoyable part of the kayak fishing ritual.

A BRIEF NOTE ON INVASIVE SPECIES

Many nonnative species of plant and animal life are invading our waterways. All boat-based fishermen, not just kayak anglers, must take some responsibility in helping to ensure that we're not carriers of species such as milfoil or zebra mussels. Kayaks have a very small imprint on the ecosystem as it is, but we can ensure that footprint remain small by thoroughly washing our kayaks, paddles, and anchors each time we return home from a fishing trip and letting the vessel completely dry before heading into a new waterway. It's easy to do, doesn't take much effort, and should always be an integral part of the return trip home.

Part Three

Kayak Fishing Paddling Skills

Even panfish offer a good challenge to kayak anglers.

Flip That Kayak

Have you already had the kayak out on the water? Maybe you even took a fishing rod or two with you. Perhaps you even caught a fish! Congratulations. If you're like me, you probably already think you're an expert kayak fisherman. After all, you paddled your kayak, and you caught a fish. Mission accomplished. Also, if you're like me, you likely skipped an important step. It's so important, in fact, that (here we go again) it might save your life.

You need to flip your kayak.

Preferably before your first outing, you need to find a nice safe place like a sandy beach on a small body of water or (don't laugh) a nearby swimming pool. If you use a pool, I'd suggest it either be yours or someone you know, so as not to cause problems and unnecessary contact with law enforcement officials. With your proving ground secured, remove everything from your kayak except your paddle and paddle leash. Everything. Donning your PFD, walk your kayak out into waist-deep water, capsize it, and try to get back on. Flip it right-side up, and then try to climb aboard. You're going to find that, especially while wearing a PFD, this does not come naturally. There are many methods for climbing aboard a capsized kayak, and not a single one of them that is easy. That's why it's imperative to practice this multiple times (preferably on multiple outings) in good weather and warm (or warmish) water. After the shallow water practice, it's advisable to attempt this "self-rescue" in water that's up to your chest, then up to your neck. Because there is always a chance of banging your head even during these practices, it's never recommended that you do this in water over your head. The "over your head" part, which entails a lot of water that you'll likely be fishing, can easily be simulated in neck-deep water by simply treading water.

SOT kayaks make things a bit easier. When I first started reading reviews of sit-inside kayaks, the SOT guys made it sound like self-rescue in an SIK was impossible. It is not impossible, but it requires practice. Both types of boats require practice for self-rescue. I can't emphasize this enough: it is not easy. Being a bit more stable, and with a more accessible platform, the SOT kayak is definitely the easier of the two on which to perform a self-rescue. There are many, many methods. I'll touch on a few of them here, but I must emphasize to you that reading about them on paper and committing them to memory is no substitute for practice. Even real water practice is no substitute for the panic that will set in should you actually capsize your kayak (known as "turtling") in icy water far from shore. That's why practice under ideal conditions is so important. *It could save your life.*

There are several methods of reentering a flipped SOT kayak. The first step in any of them is righting a flipped kayak. This part may seem easy but, particularly in water over your head (or close to it), you simply don't have the leverage to easily pull this off and will be shocked at how difficult it is to just get this first step completed before you can even *attempt* self-rescue. That big, stable boat will work against your efforts to flip it back over. Many experts now recommend a length of rope attached to a cleat or a side-handle of your kayak somewhere near the middle to aid in this very important step. The rope or strap is often needed to aid in gripping it with wet hands under less than ideal circumstances. Only practice with *your* kayak will tell you if that is necessary, or if your boat is easy enough to flip back over without an aid.

Practice it!

After righting the kayak, the next step is to climb aboard. Without a doubt, the most popular way to self-rescue on an SOT fishing kayak is the stern entry. This involves simply pushing the back end of the kayak down and climbing aboard, usually by flopping your belly onto the stern platform and pulling yourself forward or crawling to the seat. There are many methods. You'll find several videos on YouTube demonstrating the various methods, such as the Cowboy Method, to help you visualize these steps. Some of the other methods require flopping your body across the kayak's midsection. Done carefully, this can work very well, but, unlike the stern entry method, a moment's imbalance can send you right back over the opposite side and also risk flipping the kayak again. The stern entry method allows more leeway in keeping the kayak

This is not how you want your fishing trip to end. Practicing for the unexpected is a kayak angling necessity.

upright, which, chances are, you worked very hard to do in the first place. With the side entry, you won't have to crawl along the length of the kayak to get back into the seat, but it may take a little more effort (and practice!) to master this. There is at least one "rescue ladder" on the market to aid in the side entry (though it could also be used for stern entry). It's simply a length of rope tied to the side handle or a cleat near the seat, often with a small PVC step. It hangs about three feet below the boat when pulled into the water and gives a single step to aid in getting up into the kayak. As with any reentry, this requires stretching your upper body across to the far side of the kayak as the entry is attempted to prevent another flip. I've seen DIY versions of the rescue ladder made simply from a piece of rope with a loop in the end. I'm sure that would work fine, too. These straps and loops can be shoved under the seat, as long as they are accessible after flipping your boat. Don't store them in an inner hatch!

As I mentioned earlier, I was scared off of SIK fishing kayaks early on by the SOT guys' claims that you couldn't reenter an SIK in deep water, if need be, to perform a self-rescue. While it's true that an SOT with its open floor plan is a more ideal setup, you can indeed self-rescue in an SIK. It requires practice! A capsized SIK will take on water, but, as long as it has built-in floating aids such as foam blocks or sealed bulkheads (they all do now), the kayak can be righted and paddled back to shore. Unlike whitewater kayaks, which often have a spray skirt and can be "rolled" while sitting inside in the event of a capsize, SIK angling kayaks often have an open cockpit, relatively speaking. The chances are very good that you will just fall out of it if the boat goes over. At this point, you need to self-rescue. In what is known as a "wet reentry" you should, facing the stern, put your head into the cockpit from underwater. You'll find an air pocket there in which you can breathe. Place your paddle on your strongest side (typically your right side if you are right-handed) and hold it tight against the upper side of the cockpit (known as the coaming). Place both hands on the coaming and roll your legs between your arms. Slide into the kayak. Get into the seat. You are now facing forward, but underwater. Start the roll with your paddle. You may overcompensate and capsize again, since a waterlogged kayak is very unstable, but try rolling again. Do not panic (easier said than done). Once you are upright, water should immediately be removed from the kayak. Splashing it out with your hands can work in a pinch, but having a bailer of some type (such as a milk jug with the sides cut down, or even a bait pail) will aid in getting the water out and getting you back to dry land more quickly. There are hand pumps available that can do the job, but they aren't necessary. A pail or jug will likely work faster.

Scared yet? Don't be. Please keep in mind, at this point, a paddling instructor can be invaluable, but, whether in an SOT or an SIK, you *can* rescue yourself. As mentioned in the opening paragraphs of this chapter, you must practice this with your kayak under calm conditions in warm water. It can really be fun, if you like to swim. The point is that you get comfortable with getting back in your boat under ideal circumstances, so you're familiar with how everything works when you're panicking the first time you swamp your kayak. And you might.

Sooner or later, you may find yourself overboard.

Plan ahead. Try it a few times. If you have trouble righting the kayak, put a strap onboard to assist. If you simply cannot heave yourself over the edge of the kayak, use a rope with a loop or a commercial rescue ladder. DIY is perfectly fine here. It's just a rope threaded through a piece of PVC pipe. With no DIY skills at all, you can make the ladder that saves your life in about three minutes.

Also keep in mind that, though you've practiced self-rescue with an empty kayak, in real life, you'll probably have obstacles. A fish finder near the seat may catch your PFD. The PFD can snag on *everything*. Those rods that you carefully secured with rod leashes may now become multiple underwater obstacles around which you must maneuver. All of this may happen in cold water, maybe with a hook stuck in your foot, while the paddle leash has wrapped around your leg, and you are in a blind panic not only over your own safety, but over the fact that you lost some valuable gear overboard.

Focus.

Your survival depends on your focus. Practice and practice some more. And, under the right conditions, the practice can be fun. And if you *do* go overboard, at best, you have a story to tell. At worst, you may have lost some gear. Gear can be replaced. *You* cannot. Practice-flipping and self-rescue in your kayak is a very important part of becoming a successful, confident kayak angler. The more confidence you have, the more you will enjoy this sport. The previous chapter regarding clothing comes into play here. If you've properly "dressed to swim," you have nothing to worry about if it takes a few tries to get back on your boat. This is very important: Do not, under any circumstances, remove your PFD during self-rescue! It may be a hindrance in getting back aboard, but it may also save your life if things go awry.

This chapter is not intended to worry you about the prospect of bobbing in the water next to your kayak. It happens. Rather, it's meant to remind you that it *can happen.* It may *never* happen, but if it does, it's great comfort to know that you've practiced getting back on board, and that you have a better than average chance of getting back home to your family.

Planning Your First Outing

Let's presume your first outing in your new fishing kayak will be during daylight hours. It should be. In a later chapter, we'll talk about night paddling and night fishing, and the various ways angling kayaks can be rigged to provide light to you and to other boats you may encounter after dark. For now, let's talk about how to prepare for your maiden voyage.

FILE A FLIGHT PLAN

Make this a habit each and every time you leave your home. Whether it's an email to your family, a text, or a note on the refrigerator, you should always specify *exactly* where you will be launching and where you plan to fish. I'm sure you're getting tired of me saying this by now, but it could save your life. If you were to go over in cold water and a family member only knew that you'd be launching at your favorite spot, rescuers could be delayed. If they

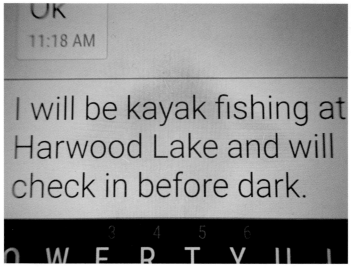

File a flight plan.

knew that you'd be headed north, upstream into the upper reaches of the creek, the time it takes to find you will be greatly reduced. With modern technology, we almost always have cell phones with us. If your plans change midstream (literally), simply send a text saying, "Change in plans—I decided to head south out to the lake." It only takes a moment out of your fishing day, but it's a very important piece of communication for your loved ones to have. I do this whether I'm hunting or fishing, every single time.

SPARE PADDLE

Pick up an inexpensive spare paddle and put it somewhere on your kayak that you can access without a lot of effort. There are very cheap, telescoping single-bladed paddles that can be had at a discount store for less than fifteen dollars. Keep it with you at all

An emergency paddle can save the day.

times. Even with a paddle leash, there's always a risk of losing your paddle. In wind or current, your primary paddle (even if it floats) can get away from you very quickly. Your cheap little backup paddle can mean the difference between continuing on with your day of fishing or being completely stranded. There are currently some one-handed fishing paddles designed for auxiliary movement without having to grab your primary paddle to make small positioning adjustments while you are fishing. These would also be an adequate solution to fill the need for a spare paddle.

PFD

Since we spent an entire chapter discussing PFDs, simply don't forget to take your PFD and *wear it!*

Your PFD should not only be with you, but on you.

CELL PHONE

Carry your cell phone on the water with you. There are a million and one types of dry bags and boxes, some of which are designed specifically for cell phones. A Ziploc sandwich bag will work in a pinch, if you've run out of kayak-fishing budget at this juncture.

In your phone, save emergency numbers, including the number of the US Coast Guard office nearest to your fishing destination.

Cell phones are the bane of society at times, and I recommend you leave your ringer off (if not your entire phone) at all times when you're fishing; but, at the same time, having one on board may (here we go) *save your life*. Seriously.

PADDLE LEASH

No, this one won't save your life, wise guy. But it will save your paddle. Paddle leashes are simply a length of thin bungee or shock cord, typically attached to the paddle with a strip of Velcro and

A paddle leush Is a safety necessity.

to the kayak at a cleat, seat, or anything else you choose to loop it through. Other high-end paddle leashes can be retractable and/or permanently attached to the kayak. When fishing, you'll be surprised how often you quickly drop your paddle to set the hook or grab your rod. I promise you this: you *will* drop your paddle overboard, and your surest way to retrieve it will be to still have it attached to your kayak via your paddle leash. When I bought my first kayak, I paid twelve dollars for a paddle leash, opened the package, and knew I'd been had. I then bought fifty feet of stretch cord for a few dollars and a roll of strip Velcro and for less than ten dollars had the makings for dozens of paddle leashes. In the paddle leash department, I highly recommend DIY. If you have the money to burn, please just send it to me, care of Skyhorse Publishing.

SAFETY REQUIREMENTS

As of this writing, the US Coast Guard has very little in the way of regulations governing what must be carried on a kayak. While other, larger boats have a bevy of required gear, kayaks do not. But the USCG is not the only governing body, and your home state may have its own requirements. Lights (at least a good flashlight), flare-gun, throwable PFD, tow rope, cell phone, and/or radio are all excellent additions to the kayak angler's safety gear selection. For any fisherman, a basic first aid kit is a necessity. I also personally recommend a good sheath knife. If your anchor hangs up on the bottom, a good sharp knife can be invaluable to get you out of a potentially dangerous situation.

Follow the federal and local requirements and use a good dose of common sense. Water, food, and sunscreen are all good ideas to have along on your first paddling trip, depending on the length of your day.

WEATHER

Before heading out on your first voyage, keep a close eye on the weather forecast. Even the calmest days and the flattest water can erupt into sudden wind and waves. This is a good practice for each

A weather app on your phone can keep you ahead of incoming storms.

and every kayak angling adventure you undertake and is especially important when you're new to the sport and unfamiliar with handling your kayak in adverse conditions.

IN SUMMATION

Very soon, we're going to talk about paddling and rigging your kayak for angling. This chapter is just a brief look at the basics. These are the things you need to go out on the water and take that thing for a spin. File your flight plan with your family or friends. If you have your kayak, your PFD, paddle, *spare* paddle, paddle leash, and your cell phone, you are ready to go out on the water and get some paddling under your belt.

Some will tell you that an anchor is an absolute must for kayak fishing, and I would be one of those people. But let's just get the basics of paddling down first. I know you'll bring a rod or two along, and maybe a handful of lures, but I highly recommend that you "paddle first, fish later."

Anchors will be discussed in a later chapter (see page 209), and I also recommend that you read that chapter before messing with an anchor in your brand-new kayak. For today, let's just get you out on the water. That's *on* the water. Hopefully not *in* the water.

A little kayak humor for you.

Into the Water

When I began kayak fishing in my first sit-inside kayak, only one thing stressed me out for any length of time. It wasn't paddling, wind, waves, or powerboats (though they still spook me from time to time). What stressed me out the most was entering the kayak and shoving off. Similarly, I also worried myself while out fishing about how I would land at the launch. Had I read and researched the pages of a book such as this, I would have had some tips and tricks under my belt before stumbling and bumbling my way in and out of the kayak. I can do it pretty effortlessly now, but there's still a modicum of adventure when launching on a rocky area, or from a dock in my sit-inside. From my sit-on-top kayak, launching causes almost no stress. We'll talk about that in a bit. I didn't mention the difference between launching an SOT and an SIK in the kayak selection chapter, because now that I'm experienced in both, I don't believe that should be a deciding factor in selecting your fishing 'yak.

All of the methods listed below require practice. Once again, you should practice these on a warm day, with your kayak emptied of valuable gear and tackle. In a short hour or two, you'll quickly

Launching quickly and efficiently is a skill you should master.

gain the confidence needed to get your fishing 'yak in and out of the water in an efficient manner.

Practice, practice, practice, and practice some more.

LAUNCHING AND LANDING AN SIK FROM A DOCK

At first blush, launching from a dock seems very simple. Just drag or carry your kayak to the dock, slide it in, and step down into it. Right?

No.

Honestly, with a sit-inside, I find dock launching the most hair-raising, counterintuitive way to get your SIK in the water. Give me a beach, creek bank, or ramp any day. The problem with dock launching is that brief moment in which your weight is transferred from the dock to the kayak. It's not as simple as stepping into a boat. You must lower yourself (often quite far down) into the seated position. There is *always* a point at which your weight is *not* centered over the kayak. There's also always a risk that you'll plop down in your seat off-center at the moment of release and end up capsizing the boat. Dock entry is a much drier way to enter your SIK than other methods, but not if you end up swimming.

Some methods of SIK dock entry include using the paddle as a brace, holding it against the coaming and perpendicular to the dock. (This method works very well for beach and bank launching, as well.) Think of the paddle as an outrigger. The important piece of this technique is the firm grip you employ to hold the paddle against the coaming. If that fails, expect chaos to ensue.

With your weight firmly over the dock, lower yourself gently into the kayak while slowly twisting your hips to slide your legs up into the cockpit. Using your arm strength for stability (as well as possibly your paddle, if you so choose), slowly transition your head over the center of the kayak. Lower yourself into the seat with your arms. As soon as you are stable, push *gently* off from the dock. Too many people capsize their boats *at* the dock by giving a mighty shove. It's not necessary, and very ill-advised. The paddle can be used to push off as well but, again, *gently*. The paddle can give added leverage, but this is not an instance in which that additional leverage is necessarily a good thing.

Landing at a dock with an SIK also requires some planning, but it can be done safely and effectively. After (slowly) approaching the dock to arm's length, carefully lean your shoulders toward the dock, while keeping your head over the center of the kayak. The paddle may be pinned again against the coaming and over the dock for stabilization, but I have as yet to find a dock that perfectly matches the height of any given angling kayak. The paddleless method involves leaning, then beginning to pull yourself up onto the dock while pulling your knees to a slightly bent position and out of the kayak. More weight on your arms is what makes this technique much easier. Upper body strength is a great asset when launching and landing your kayak at a dock. Putting weight on your feet or standing in your kayak at this point is a recipe for disaster. Your body should remain low, or crouched, at all times until you're safely on the dock. At that point, use your bow tow rope or handle to pull the boat up onto the dock, and you're on your way.

LAUNCHING AND LANDING AN SIK FROM BEACHES, BANKS, AND RAMPS

There are a hundred and one ways to safely launch an SIK from a beach. For our purposes, we'll call a beach not only a sandy area, but a mucky, grassy, or pebbly area without an overabundance of big rocks.

If you have a partner handy, simply place your boat into the water nose first, have the partner stabilize the boat near the stern, and get in. Some kayak enthusiasts prefer a drier launch, involving more pushing off from the beach with arms (both arms in the water, for stability) or pushing off with the paddle, particularly in colder conditions. But if you're launching with a partner, they can also shove you off. *Gently.*

Another way to launch solo is to position the kayak as mentioned above and to straddle the boat and walk to the cockpit, finally lowering yourself into the seat. This is a great way to enter the kayak, because your body is balanced over the center of the kayak for the entirety of the operation. This can be done with the kayak mostly on the beach, mostly on the water, or a combination of both. It all depends on how wet you want your feet to get. Personally, I don't like starting out wet in my SIK and usually prefer a bit drier launch, often with two-thirds of the kayak on the dry bank, and using my paddle or arms to push or shimmy the kayak the rest of the way into the water.

The previously mentioned paddle bracing for dock launching is also an excellent way to enter the kayak from the beach or bank.

Instead of the kayak being positioned perpendicular to the water, it is positioned parallel. Extend the paddle to the bank or beach and clamp your hand around the paddle on the coaming. Done correctly, this method stabilizes the kayak for a rock-solid entry. As mentioned above, a firm grip on the paddle and coaming are very important. When I launch my SIK, this is how I typically do it.

In rockier areas, or streams with steeper banks, I prefer the paddle-bracing method. With just a little practice, this can be mastered. It eliminates the stress of worrying about taking a bath when entering or exiting the kayak and leads to a more relaxed day of fishing.

For ramp launches, any of the above methods can be used, but you'll want to keep in mind that a concrete ramp is more likely to damage your boat than a beach or bank. It's advisable to have more of your kayak in the water to prevent scraping plastic on concrete.

Kayak launches come in all shapes and sizes from simple . . .

. . . to high-tech.

With most boat launches, there's the option of entering from the dock or walkway portion of the ramp. I'm advising against it. A dock entry will be drier in theory but allows more risk of capsizing.

In a few pages we will talk about ramp etiquette.

SOT Kayak Launching

Sit-on-top kayaks are easier to launch than SIKs in all of the scenarios listed above. With their stable, wide platforms and secondary stability, it's pretty hard to flip an SOT at the launch. (Oh yes, it can be done, but you really have to not be paying attention). Most ocean and big-water kayak anglers will be using an SOT angling kayak. Launching in surf adds a whole new (and sometimes scary) dimension to SOT kayak launching. Many new kayak anglers plunge out into the waves, assuming they're going to get wet anyway, and suddenly find themselves looking at the bottom of their boat pointed toward the sky. All of the launch tips listed for SIKs hold true with SOTs. Keeping your head positioned above the kayak's center of gravity is a *must* with surf-launching, just as much as it is with paddling, fighting fish, and even taking photos. It's simply good kayak form to keep your head centered above the kayak's centerline and keel. Balance is very important in all kayak launching.

Surf launches requires watching the waves and positioning your kayak perpendicular not necessarily to the shore, but to the incoming waves. SOT anglers generally get their boat into the surf in a few inches of water and simply step aboard. There's little concern for water getting on deck, because that will be eliminated by the scupper holes. Once stepping onto the kayak and sliding into the seat, having paid close attention to balance and center of gravity during the operation, you are ready to go. Just start paddling into the waves until you're out into a less abusive zone in the surf. This holds true for not only ocean launches, but big lakes and rivers and any body of water that sees challenging waves at the launch area.

Dock launching an SOT kayak is much easier than it is for an SIK. With their stable platform, there's more wiggle room (quite literally) when lowering your weight from the dock down to the kayak platform. There's no need to contort your legs as there is in an SIK, because there is no cockpit. Always pay attention to rod holders, fish finders, cameras, and any other gear that might catch your foot as you step onto your kayak. Holding on to the dock, keeping at least some of your weight over the dock surface until your footing is secure, is always a good idea. Start initial contact by placing your feet in a wide, even stance in the kayak. Many confident anglers with stand-up kayaks will often "walk" onto their kayaks from a dock. Before you attempt this, I must caution you that you should be entirely familiar with the stand-up capabilities of both your 'yak—and you! A dock presents many different obstacles such as pilings, rip-rap, and someone else's bass boat on which you can clock your head. Overconfidence kills, as in most of life's adventures.

Be careful!

Launching in a river, at a ramp—almost any place you can think to launch—requires planning, even in an SOT. Keep in mind

Learning to launch anywhere is a must-have kayak angling skill.

transducers that could be damaged. If you have electronics hanging off the bottom of your kayak, you'll need a bit "wetter" launch and have more of the kayak in the water before mounting the boat. In muddy conditions, you should consider doing a bit drier launch, rather than get your legs bogged down in the mucky nastiness and spending the day with your 'yak covered in slimy goop.

COMMON SENSE

Whether SOT or SIK launching, common sense goes a long way. If possible, don't launch in areas with large boulders and heavy current. Your kayak is *not* a white-water kayak, and, chances are, you are not an experienced paddler. At least not yet. Find a place free of submerged trees, overhanging low branches, and other obstacles. You want to avoid the possibility of damaging the bottom of the boat as well as low overhead clearances that could damage your fishing rods, camera mounts, and safety flags.

RAMP ETIQUETTE

Oh boy. I could write a book on this from the things I've seen over the years, from canoeists, to bass boats, to big charter boats and—yes—kayak fishermen. Everyone wants to get out there fishing, but sometimes things go awry. Angry glares, maybe words, are exchanged. It doesn't have to be like that!

There are no hard and fast rules regarding ramp etiquette for kayak fisherman. But, chances are, if you are using a public launch, you're sharing the ramp with a host of other nonkayak fishermen who are all just as interested in getting to their favorite fishing spot as quickly as (or more quickly than) you. Kayak fishermen are increasing in numbers, and sometimes one or two of us will elicit groans from the bigger power boat guys as we make

Try to avoid submerged roots and other obstacles when launching and landing.

trip after trip from our car to the boat and hold up ramp progress. Similarly, I've seen kayak guys complain about the wakes
and other challenges presented by sharing the water with those
big, scary boats.

Can't we all just get along? Sure we can.

I'm a kayak guy, but I've also been a boat guy. The bottom line is that we all need to do our thing efficiently. Get the boat in the water, get your gear on the boat, and get out of the way so the next guy can have his turn. Whether you're a kayak fisherman or a big-boat person, these are the unwritten rules of ramp etiquette. And they are just that simple.

As kayak anglers, we can do our part to keep things moving. Once the boat is unloaded at the ramp, stash your gear quickly off to the side (or very quickly into the boat) and get your vehicle out of the way. Since I've moved into kayak trailering, I've reduced the stress of this part greatly, since everything can be kept on the boat or, at the very least, loaded into the boat before backing down to the water. But even the car-top guys, or the truck-bed guys, need to load and unload efficiently. And then move your car out of the way.

Observe proper ramp etiquette . . .

Remember the Soup Nazi on *Seinfeld*? You have to keep moving, and everything will be okay. Stop, hold up a line of trailers waiting to get to the ramp, and guess what. *No soup for you!*

Be organized! The launch is not the area where you should be searching for misplaced gear, organizing your tackle, rigging your rods, or any other activity that is sure to attract the ire of the guy behind you waiting to launch his eighty-thousand-dollar cruiser. Get your gear organized at home, in the parking lot before you head down to the ramp, or, if need be, when you get out on the water. Don't let your lack of preparation be the reason that people start hurling beer bottles at you to get you moving. (I've never really seen that happen, but close . . .)

Condense your gear into what can be carried in a minimal number of trips. A dry bag, a crate, and your rods should be all you need. Make it all fit. If it doesn't, stow some of the gear in the inner hatches ahead of your trip and leave it there. Typically, the lightest gear is left in the boat to make it easier to carry or car-top, while the

. . . and don't block the ramp for any longer than necessary.

heavier stuff can be ferried down to the water's edge once the boat has been dropped by the water.

If the area permits, move your kayak off to the side of the actual ramp. There's no reason to have your kayak in the middle of the ramp if you could just as easily be loading it up out of the way of the people behind you. Better yet, don't use the ramp at all if there's a convenient area nearby to do a beach launch. We kayak anglers have options that larger boats do not have.

Once you've launched, get the kayak out of the launch area. This is for your own safety and the mental well-being of your fellow ramp fishermen. If you're out of the way, there's less reason you might get reprimanded and/or "educated."

I'm a big fan of treating strangers as I'd treat a friend. Be kind, courteous, and use a little common sense, and you'll find that there's plenty of room at the ramp (and on the water) for all of us.

Paddling Form

This isn't a book on paddling. There are plenty of them out there if you are interested in the intricacies of the activity. You can learn about different strokes (for different folks), energy efficiency, drag, and a host of other technical terms. Or you can just go kayaking and see what happens. With your paddle likely being the primary propulsion system of your fishing kayak, it doesn't hurt to have at least some rudimentary knowledge of good form. Can you just jump into the boat and start paddling? Sure you can. I'm guessing—just maybe—that you already did. That's what I did, and I did okay. But when I learned just a few finer points of kayak paddling, I found it easier to move those big, heavy, cost-effective boats that I touted earlier in this book. Kayak paddling isn't hard. You can just jump in and go and there's a chance that you'll develop good form, but it's also possible that you will ingrain some bad habits. Those bad habits can hurt your ultimate goal of getting out on the water and catching fish while staying pain free. So let's just take a quick rundown—without getting too technical—of a few things that can make the kayaking portion of kayak angling just a little more enjoyable.

HEAD POSITION

So much of good kayak angling has to do with your head. Not just the stuff inside your head that aids in good decision making and planning, but your actual noggin, pumpkin, or brain bucket. Proper balance when entering or exiting your kayak is heavily dependent on your head being centered in the kayak. Similarly, playing or landing large fish also depends on good head position, as we'll discuss in that chapter. *Where the head goes, the body follows* is a common theme touted by kayak experts. In other words, if your head is out over the side of the boat, so may you be very soon. But head position also plays a critical role in the paddling portion of the program.

When paddling, your head should remain not only balanced in the center of the kayak for stability, but also upright and looking

Good paddling form includes proper head position and good paddling posture.

forward. Tired kayakers tend to find their chin sinking to their chests as they plow forward. Don't let this happen to you. It will only serve to exacerbate the pain and increase the fatigue. Hold your head up high and keep good posture at all times. This will reduce fatigue and eliminate the chance of developing neck pain.

ARMS AND SHOULDERS

Most inexperienced kayak paddlers *pull* themselves through the water with their arm muscles, imagining that they are pulling the water toward them. This is incorrect. In a correct kayak stroke, your arm muscles should not play a large role in the movement. This seems counterintuitive because, after all, you're holding the paddle with your arms, right? Not exactly.

Instead of bending your elbows and dragging the paddle toward you, you should rather pivot at the waist and rotate your

Paddling with proper torso rotation will reduce arm fatigue on challenging days.

shoulders. This allows the larger muscles of your upper body to do the majority of the work. This is the magic ingredient in paddling heavy fishing kayaks, as well. With your arms freed up from a large portion of that pulling motion, you'll find that your arms will feel better over the course of the day. They simply aren't being strained as much. This is a key point that new kayak anglers should keep in mind. Paddling that boat full of gear (even the superlight models) across even a modest-sized lake is a workout. It should not, however, be an *arm* workout. Correct paddling form will allow you to save your arms for hauling that forty-pound pike up on deck for its close-up.

Another typical beginner's paddling mistake involves raising the off-hand (the side of the paddle that's not in the water) too high. It's not necessary to dig the paddle deeply into the water and also unnecessary to raise your off-hand way up to achieve it. Deep paddle gouging reduces efficiency, and raising the off-hand up is unnecessary movement that is fatiguing. Just like you'll want to develop economy when you load your tackle boxes for your kayak, you also need to develop economy of motion when it comes to paddling. Unnecessary movements add up over the course of a day fishing and paddling and contribute to unnecessary levels of fatigue.

LEGS, BACK, AND POSTURE

Proper positioning of your legs is very important. In an SIK, you don't have many options. Is it starting to sound like I am anti-SIK? No, far from it. On longer days on the water, however, an SOT allows for much better posture. In an SIK, your legs are at the same level as your hips, and blood flow is greatly reduced. Stopping and periodically stretching is a necessity, at least for someone my age. An SOT allows proper blood flow to the legs as well as the ability to move around a bit more. This alleviates stress on the legs, hips, and back. SOTs also typically have a more ergonomic seat, which itself improves your posture without much effort on your part. The back support built into a modern SOT kayak seat is one of the true blessings of this advancing technology.

Good kayak paddling posture (this holds true for fishing as well) requires holding your back straight (*sit up straight,* as your mom might say) and having your behind planted firmly against the back of the seat. Knees should be slightly bent, and your foot pegs should be adjusted to accommodate exactly that position. Your large leg muscles should lock you into that paddling position. The more firmly you are engaged with the boat, the easier and more efficient your paddling will be. If you're slipping around with your legs, or your backside is squirming in your seat, you're losing precious energy that could have gone into propelling the kayak forward. Efficiency is what it's all about, and, if you have a rock-solid foundation, you will have paddling efficiency.

Again, this is not intended to be a primer on paddling, but a few tips to get you started in the right direction. Keep your head centered and upright. Pivot at the waist to form your paddle stroke. Wait until the paddle has engaged the water to begin your stroke, but resist the urge to *dig* into the water. Let your hip rotation and the paddle do the work. Keep your legs slightly bent, but locked into the pegs. Keep your back firmly against the back of the seat. Off you go. Paddling really is simple. Later on, we'll chat about paddling in current and discuss a few alternate paddling methods for windy days, but keep these basics in mind on your first open-water trip, and you'll be ahead of the game. Keep it fun and comfortable, and you'll find it enjoyable. And as with everything else we've discussed in these pages, if it's enjoyable, you're doing it right.

Stand-Up Paddling and Fishing

So, you selected an angling 'yak that has stand-up capabilities? I'm not surprised, since many current fishing kayaks tout this feature. There are many advantages to the ability to stand and paddle or stand up and fish. Obviously, a higher angle to the water increases visibility for not only sighting fish, but also underwater obstacles. When it comes to hooking fish, the higher angle will increase your successful hook sets. Also, when fighting fish, the ability to lift a fish's head out of the slop is a great advantage. Much like a kayak angler, where the fish's head goes, so their body follows. It's also a good way to stretch and reduce back fatigue. There are countless advantages to standing up in your kayak.

How hard is standing up on a fishing kayak? It depends on you. It also depends on the kayak. I've found everything about kayak fishing to be easier than I initially expected. Standing up and balancing on a floating kayak is not hard. That said, it's not as straightforward or (dare I say) easy as you might be led to believe. This is one of the areas of kayak angling for which practice before

Stand-up kayak angling adds a new dimension and added fishing visibility.

hitting the water, as well as on the water, is invaluable. Much like self-rescue, stand-up paddling and fishing is well worth a couple of hours invested in practicing.

What helps make standing up in your stand-up kayak easier? Most stand-up models come with a pull-up strap. It's simply a strap centered ahead of the seat, which is designed to have your arm strength aid you in getting upright. If your boat didn't come with a pull-up strap, one can easily be fashioned from a discount store dog leash and a well-secured cleat. Just make sure you get the type of leash designed for big dogs, unless you only weigh as much as a Pomeranian.

Another aid in getting yourself standing in a kayak is to have your seat (if it's adjustable) adjusted to its highest possible setting before attempting to stand. If your seat is fixed-height, the higher it is, the easier you'll find to get yourself upright. Boat stability is, of course, a big factor in successful stand-up kayak activities; but,

The "stand-assist" strap on a standard stand-up SOT kayak.

if the boat is marketed as a stand-up kayak, there should be more than enough stability on hand. Finally, good physical condition, including upper body and leg strength and relative overall fitness, will aid greatly in your stand-up fishing and paddling endeavors. Not to put too fine a point of it, but if you have trouble standing up in your living room, you might find standing in a kayak a bit too much of a challenge. And that's okay, too. Standing on a kayak is not for everyone, and it's certainly not necessary for a good day of kayak angling.

PRACTICE ON DRY LAND

If your kayak has a deep keel, brace it with pillows or sand bags or whatever you have handy so it is resting evenly (and solidly) on the ground. Sit in your seat as if you were fishing or paddling. For the first exercise, have your hands free and set your paddle out of the way. Hold the pull-up strap in both of your hands. Pull your feet toward you as far as you can. Take an evenly spaced, wide stance with your feet flat on the deck. Pull yourself upright using both your arms and your legs. Don't move too quickly, but don't spend too much time "in between," either. You'll quickly figure out what works best for you. That's what practice is all about.

To sit back down, bend your legs, taking care to keep your feet evenly spaced, and lower yourself down to the seat, landing squarely on the seat as much as possible. Avoid the natural tendency to place your hand or hands on the seat below you. This is a recipe for disaster. If you land slightly off-center, you can quickly correct, but not if your hand is in the way. Keep your hands off the seat and off the boat until you are back in the seat.

Practice getting up and down as many times as you can. When you're ready for a change of pace, practice picking up your rod while standing, then your paddle. Then practice switching the two. Whether standing or sitting, you'll be amazed at how many times you perform the rod-paddle-rod swap during a fishing outing. These movements should become natural and familiar, and dry land is a great place to practice them.

This practice is invaluable and it will get you far ahead of the game before you attempt . . .

WATER PRACTICES

Follow the same steps listed above in the dry-land practice. The only difference is that you're going to practice all of the same moves in a few inches to a foot of water. Do this on a warm day, in warm-water conditions. Keep your feet spread wide at all times. Use the strap. Do not use your hands on the seat for standing *or* sitting. Be mindful of your kayak rigging, such as rod holders and electronics, and keep your strap and your feet clear of them at all times.

Once you've practiced standing and sitting several times, stand up. Holding on to your stand-up strap, rock the boat. Gently at first, use hip-action and your feet to test your kayak's stability. You may find that you can rock the kayak much farther than you'd anticipated, due to its built-in secondary stability. Or you may find that your kayak is less stable than you imagined. If that's the case, you may find yourself sitting or standing in a few inches of water with no damage done, other than your pride. This is the time to prove to yourself how far you can push your kayak's stability in a stand-up situation. These shallow-water lessons are invaluable. It's the only way you'll find your limitations. But, more important, they are the only way in which you will build confidence in what you'll be able to realistically expect and achieve when stand-up angling.

Once your confidence has grown, while still in shallow water, once again practice picking up your paddle and switching that for your fishing rod. Without the stability of dry land and your center of gravity far above what it is while sitting in the kayak, you'll soon

Stand-up paddling is a skill every stand-up kayak angler should practice.

get a feel for the slow, steady motions needed for stand-up maneuvers. You'll find that, much like carrying a full glass of water, if you look to the horizon, rather than into the boat, it's much easier to maintain balance.

GETTING DEEPER

Once you've practiced in shallow water, remain standing and try paddling out into a few feet of water. You'll get the feel for using the paddle at a steeper angle. Practice turning the boat, but go slowly at first, as the additional torque of the paddle in the water will have an effect on your balance. Slowly, slowly. Get a feel for it. If you've purchased or made a push-pole, this is the time to try it. Carefully switch the paddle for the pole, always taking care to keep your feet anchored and equidistant, and practice poling in the still relatively shallow water. *Be careful!* You'll find that sometimes the pole gets stuck in muck or weeds. Don't force it. Don't do *anything* that quickly shifts your balance. If the pole gets hung up, keep your head centered (always!) over the kayak and lift firmly with *one hand* until it comes loose. Don't sacrifice your stability on the 'yak for speed. If the push-pole gets really hung up, carefully sit down (no hands!) and attempt to retrieve it from the seated position. The same holds true with anchors, and with landing big fish. These are two of several balance-tossing activities for which it's much safer and simpler to take a moment, sit down, and deal with them from a more secure position and a lower center of gravity.

With practice, you'll learn to turn around while standing in your kayak. It's all about even distribution of weight, and avoiding having both feet lined up in the center of the kayak, dangerously focusing your balance over too small of an area. Wide stance, wide stance, wide stance. Practice facing forward until you are much more comfortable with that. Facing backward isn't that valuable a skill. Learning to *cast* back over your shoulder will eliminate any need you may feel to face the stern. And practice casting in shallow water might get you a fish.

Again, practice switching paddle for rod, rod for paddle, paddle for stand-up pole, and practice casting. Stand and sit a few more times. I'd recommend several hours of this practice, even if it's over the course of several weeks. There is no rush to stand while kayak angling, and you should be fully comfortable with it before venturing out into deeper water or under rougher conditions.

One last tip regarding learning to stand-up in your angling kayak: it's always imperative that you watch for underwater obstacles such as tree stumps, roots, rocks, and other underwater hazards. While stand-up kayaking, it's even more important to watch for these dangers. With the higher center of gravity, what might just have been a "bump" in the road while sitting and kayaking becomes a larger problem while standing; a slight tap on the bow

Stand and deliver (the fish)! And don't forget to practice.

or stern (or anywhere!) can tip your kayak so quickly that you'll have no time to react. Watch for dangers! You'll have a better vantage point—use it! If you do find yourself suddenly running up on an object, the very best thing you can do is to grab your strap and try to get in the seated position as quickly as possible. Get that center of gravity down—now! Trying to stabilize a kayak that's suddenly run up on an object while standing will almost certainly result in overcompensation and loss of balance. Loss of balance leads to . . . well . . . you know. As with all aspects of kayak angling, preparation, common sense, and planning for danger are all part of the game.

Chances are good that you'll find stand-up kayaking to be as thoroughly enjoyable as I do, but please follow the tips above to help ensure you don't learn the right way the hard way.

Paddling in Current

I'm not going to mess around in this chapter. If you're planning on kayak angling in anything that even *resembles* white water, I'm going to suggest that you seriously consider taking a course from a professional in the field of kayaking. Most angling kayaks are not designed with the kind of maneuvering capabilities that allow for the quick turns and crosscurrent situations that are found in very fast water. That said, some new angling models are being designed for swift water and even white water. Even so, just because you are in a white-water kayak, it doesn't mean you know how to white-water kayak. I highly recommend learning from a professional or, at the very least, from another seasoned kayak angler who has been there, done that, and has the ability to properly teach you the ropes. I'm not a white-water fisherman and won't presume to tell you that I can advise you in that regard.

Most of my kayak angling has been in a small Great Lakes tributary. There are varying degrees of current, depending on how far up in the trib I decide to paddle. One tactic I truly enjoy is paddling through some current, beaching the kayak, and getting out to wade, especially during our steelhead and salmon runs. Here are

Paddling in current may become a necessity, but it's necessary to practice this skill.

a few tips that I can pass along from my own experience in dealing with current and the challenges (and fun) it presents when paddling a large angling kayak.

TWO IS BETTER THAN ONE

If you're going to go river angling in fast water, consider going with a partner. The buddy system is an age-old tried-and-true method of tackling difficult adventures. Having a friend to help you secure a capsized kayak, to call for help, or to render any other imaginable kind of aid is always a good plan.

The added advantage to swift-water angling with a partner is the ability to leave a vehicle at the takeout place and make a nice, one-way trip down the stream or river without having to contemplate paddling back up against the current to get to your vehicle. These are some of my favorite trips.

The buddy system is a good idea for new and unfamiliar waters.

LAUNCH AND LAND IN A PLACE OF CALM

Launch your kayak in a backwater, eddy, or quiet tributary. Don't attempt to launch immediately into the fast, main current unless that is the absolutely *only* way to do it. If it is the only option, refer to the buddy system above and have your partner stabilize your kayak. Similarly, when taking out, don't attempt to do it in heavy, direct current. Look for a calm eddy or even the relative shelter of the downstream side of a large boulder or any other breakwater. Be careful! Having your kayak moving beneath you in the current adds an entirely new dimension to launching and landing. Plan each of your movements carefully. Move decisively, but not before you've decided precisely what each of your moves is going to be.

LASH IT DOWN!

In our rigging chapter (see page 223), we'll talk specifics about securing gear in your angling 'yak. For now, suffice it to say that in moving water things can happen quickly and there's a greater chance of losing your gear. In addition to the hazards you may encounter in moving water, such as boulders, logs, and strainers (downed trees, etc.), there are often additional obstacles in the form of overhead branches. No matter what your water looks like, whether a calm farm pond or a relatively fast river current or even the ocean, lashing your gear down is almost always a necessity, at least to some degree. In river or stream current, it's imperative.

If you have a large SOT, chances are there is plenty of storage space belowdecks. If you're planning a river run, more gear than normal should be placed there, out of the way. The gear you do need abovedeck should all be secured. This means strapping down coolers, crates, and tackle boxes, as well as ensuring that your paddle leash is in good shape and (this is very important) using rod leashes. Rod leashes can be a pain and slow down your fishing sometimes, but the first time you flip your boat in current or a low-hanging tree branch grabs your rod tip and tries to snatch your rod from its holder, you'll be thankful that you don't have to swim for your two-hundred-dollar fishing rod. On the subject of fishing rods, a horizontal rod holder is a great addition to any kayak. It may not be used all the time, but when going under branches or low-hanging logs, it's invaluable to have the rods lower than your shoulders.

On slow current rivers with little or no risk of overhead issues, you should secure your gear just as you normally would for a day fishing. The important thing is to end the day with as much tackle and gear as you started.

When in doubt, tie it down.

In current (and almost always), gear should be well secured . . .

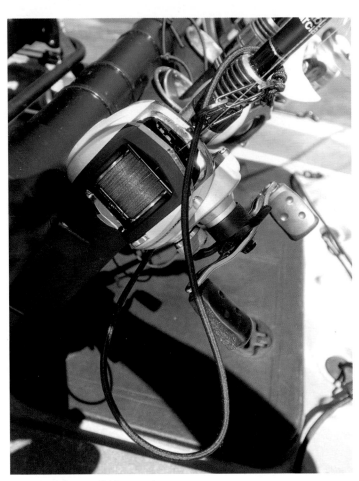

. . . especially your fishing gear!

PADDLE CONTACT

A basic tenet of kayaking is that the kayak will be more stable with the paddle in the water. This is very important in wind and waves, as well as in the current. With one end of the paddle almost constantly in the water, balance is increased. Think of the paddle as a de facto outrigger. With the current doing a large share of the work of propulsion, the paddle can be used as a rudder, and as an outrigger when steering isn't necessary.

KEEP GOOD PADDLING FORM

This is not the first, nor the last, time you will see this in these pages: *Where the head goes, so the body follows.* While paddling downstream, stay balanced and don't lose the good paddling form addressed earlier in this book. With the current doing some of the work, it's natural to let your paddling form slouch a bit. Don't! Keep your head centered, back firmly against the seat, legs slightly bent. All of the usual tips. This is important because, though you may be cruising nicely down the stream, you also may suddenly find yourself needing a power stroke to avoid a boulder, or to beach the kayak in order to avoid a strainer. Or maybe you'll just want to pause to cast at a likely-looking hole.

The ability to instantly gain control of your kayak in current is imperative. Keep good paddling form at all time, and you won't have to scramble when that obstacle suddenly appears at your bow. Speaking of which, nothing should suddenly appear at your bow! Look ahead. Wear polarized glasses to help recognize underwater hazards. All of the basic safety and form rules apply, but they apply *more* because things will happen faster in medium-to-strong current. Stay in control, and you won't have to worry about suddenly having to get back in control.

Current isn't always a big challenge, but it still pays to be aware of upcoming obstacles.

Pay attention and look ahead, even when paddling in gentle currents.

ANCHORING

Anchoring in current is a constant debate among the kayak-fishing community. Some experts will suggest it's simply too dangerous to anchor when current is present. This line of thinking is over-simplified. I'm all about kayak-angling safety, but there are many slow-moving rivers in which it's perfectly safe to drop your Bruce Claw or folding anchor, provided you follow the rules listed in the anchoring section (see page 209) and use a large dose of common sense. The danger of current anchoring lies in stronger currents and (sometimes) deeper waters. With a swift current, it's not advisable to tether yourself to the bottom of a stream. If the boat catches a bad wave, or takes a bad roll due to changing current, you can quickly find yourself under water. As mentioned in the anchoring section (see page 209), don't anchor in fast water. To the extent you're able, make sure the bottom is free of snags, boulders, and other obstructions that could snag your anchor and cause further headaches. Always, always, always utilize the anchor trolley to place the anchor near the bow or stern so the current flows around your kayak in the way for which it was designed. Current coming at your broadside while anchored is a very bad thing and will serve only to test your PFD.

PFDs

You should be wearing your PFD every minute you are on the water, so this point should be moot. However, the PFD is even more imperative in swift-water angling. Things can go bad in a big hurry in current. You don't want to be cinching up the straps on your PFD *after* you are floating down the river next to your kayak.

SELF-RESCUE

Please read and reread the earlier section on self-rescue. Self-rescue takes on a whole new meaning when dealing with river currents. If you're well practiced on getting back on board your angling kayak, you're more likely to be able to pull it off under adverse conditions such as current or wind (coming up next). River self-rescue may sometimes require that the boat be secured and dragged to the bank and into an eddy or sheltered area, and reentering from shallow water. Think ahead. Study the stream and have a plan in mind in the event that things go south.

IN SUMMATION

Paddling and angling in current is something you will want to do, at least at some point. Fish love current and anglers love fish.

Fish and current often go together. Make sure you know how to handle the current as well as the fish.

I highly recommend tackling at least a dozen flat-water trips to familiarize yourself with your kayak and your ability to control your kayak. When you do first attempt your first stream or river, go easy, think and watch ahead, and plan for the worst. You may find that your kayak is a dream in fast current. Chances are, though, that you'll realize that white-water kayaks are designed the way they are for a reason—and that reason is not fishing. And most angling kayaks were not designed with swift water in mind (again, some are!). It can be done. Don't be discouraged. Just take it slowly and learn the ins and outs before tackling fast water.

Paddling in Wind, Waves, and Weather

Paddling in current, as discussed in the last chapter, is completely up to you. You may go your whole life and never have any desire to take your angling kayak down a river or stream in which the current is more than a trickle. Paddling in wind and waves, however, is going to happen to you whether you like it or not. Unless you restrict your angling activities to one-acre farm ponds on windless days in August, sooner or later you will find yourself on a windy body of water. Because I grew up in the flat land of Western New York, wind is just a fact of life for me. Add those flat, open spaces, where the wind has a chance to gather strength over many miles, to the open bodies of water I frequently encounter like the Niagara River, Lake Erie, and Lake Ontario, and you'll know that battling wind and waves has become second nature to me. Even moderate-sized lakes have the potential for turning from calm and glassy to rough and nasty in a very short amount of time.

As a fisherman, you know that sometimes the roughest, windiest days produce fish. I'm not going to discourage you from heading out in mild or moderate winds in your angling kayak—within reason. There are some days you're going to just need to stay home, and we'll talk about those, too. In the meantime, here are a few short pointers for dealing with the inevitable wind and waves that you will encounter.

PADDLING IN WAVES AND WIND

Your kayak, even if it is a low-profile model, is not a wind-friendly vehicle. It's light, small, and easily buffeted. When paddling in wind, try to adjust your course, anticipating the direction the wind will likely take you off your heading. For example, if the wind is coming from your left, you may need to slightly quarter to the left in order to stay on course for your destination.

As I suggested in the paddling in current chapter (see page 185), all gear must be lashed down at all times to prevent loss and/or damage. You must secure your gear before paddling in wind and waves in order to ensure you end up with the same amount of stuff with which you started.

If possible, it's always a good idea to paddle into the wind at the beginning of your fishing session, and let the wind aid in bringing you back to land after you've tired from a long day fishing. Of course, that is not always possible. Some days you will find you're paddling into the wind in both directions, especially when the wind is variable, as it frequently is in my home waters. Very often you may have to paddle out downwind and return in full headwinds. Leave a little extra time if this is the case. Wind will definitely slow your progress.

With wind come waves. Perhaps one of the more difficult parts of kayak fishing on a big lake or the ocean surf is launching. We've already discussed launching in surf in the launching section (see page 160), but what I'd like to touch on here are the waves themselves. Whether lake or ocean, where the waves meet

A calm day on big water can change very quickly into challenging or even dangerous conditions.

the beach (the surf zone) is the single most difficult area in which to launch and land your kayak. When you find yourself in this zone, paddle decisively through it, keeping your kayak perpendicular to the waves at all times. Do not stop, do not anchor, and do not fish. Paddle through the surf zone as quickly and powerfully as possible. Beyond the surf zone, on a windy day, you may still encounter those big waves that are pounding the shore, but you'll soon notice that the kayak is not buffeted about as it is nearer the shore. In fact, you may find it surprising how well your kayak can handle even fairly large waves. Learning how to roll your hips with the wave action, keeping your head centered above the kayak at all times (I know, there it is again), and maintaining good paddling form will keep you on the right side of the water.

On days with waves that make it seem not even worth the effort, if you're already on the water when the wind and waves kick up, seek out the shelter of an island or the leeward side of the lake. Heavy winds can be weathered in surprisingly calm areas, if you know where to find them. Familiarity with the water you're fishing can save the day in these situations.

WATCH THE WEATHER

Watch your local weather. With the abundance of weather technology now available on your phone, as well as television and radio, there's no excuse for not being aware of upcoming fronts that often result in strong and unpredictable winds. Pay attention to any forecast that mentions a *small craft advisory.* Stay home, sharpen your fishing hooks, and polish your kayak. You do not want to be on the water during anything like a small craft advisory. Marine radios are a great investment.

Know the prevailing winds in your area. If the prevailing wind in your area is, say, a southeast wind, think hard about what it might mean if you're suddenly faced with a northwest wind. Sometimes that change in pattern can make the fish go wild, while at other times the fishing may shut down completely. What's important from a paddling perspective is that the shift away from prevailing winds often means added turbulence, especially on big water, and that can mean more and larger waves.

Since a kayak is a small craft, it can easily be hidden in the waves, often completely disappearing in large swells. Kayak anglers who frequent large bodies of water often use a flag—sometimes homemade—that extends four, five, or even six feet above the kayak. Bright colors such as orange, yellow, or fluorescent green are the best for distant visibility. Many anglers pride themselves on homemade PVC flagpoles and flags. Of course, you can buy them, too. When not needed, they can be easily stashed somewhere out of the way.

Technology keeps kayak anglers in touch with the outside world, and the incoming weather.

Anything can happen—and happen quickly—on big water.

I'm a fan of fishing during the changing fronts and have had some of my best days during the windy conditions associated with them, but follow all of the safety precautions already detailed throughout this book and keep a close eye on the weather.

Fishing in rain is another of the most productive fishing I've ever encountered. Is it that baitfish are more active, or is it the muted light? Is it just that fish love the rain (they're wet all the time, so I don't know about that . . .)? Either way, fishing during light rain or even during downpours can make for some spectacular, often competition-free, hours on the water. SOT kayaks, with their self-draining scupper holes, are ideal in the rain. SIKs, unfortunately, are not. I've sat in a puddle of water, catching fish, many times in my SIK. Bring a sponge. On an SOT, additional rainwater creates the potential hazard of a slippery deck surface. Neoprene

Scupper hole plugs may become a necessity when paddling in high waves or heavy current, but make sure to pull them if drainage becomes an issue.

booties or wading shoes can aid in traction, but be careful. Think twice or even three times about standing on a rain-slicked deck.

Beware of electrical storms. Again, watch or listen to the weather. If there's a chance of electrical storms, you do not want to be on the water in a kayak with seven six-foot rods poking up in every direction, begging for a lightning strike. Stay off the water if a storm is approaching. If you suddenly find yourself on the open water with an incoming storm, replete with rumbling thunder and distant flashes of lightning, paddle decisively back to the launch or, if time is of the essence, get to shore wherever you are and weather the lightning show on dry land. Most electrical fronts move through rather quickly, and you can resume fishing as soon as the skies clear.

Cold weather gear was mentioned earlier in this book, so I won't repeat it, but if the temps are frigid, you must dress for it as detailed in the clothing chapter (see page 108). Paddling in cold weather and snow, however, presents its own set of challenges. One of the main concerns is freezing temperatures. That water on the deck of your SOT that seemed kind of nice and refreshing in August and September can mean a slick coating of ice on your kayak deck, your paddle, your tackle, and you. If your kayak begins to ice up, it's even more imperative that you plan each move accordingly and tread very cautiously when stand-up fishing and paddling.

Paddling at Night

I've loved night fishing almost as long as I've been fishing. Fish are more active, less wary, and simply easier to catch after darkness falls. The smash of a largemouth bass taking a topwater lure in the dark is a thrill like few other. Similarly, a large trout inhaling a fly and rippling the moonlit surface is a type of magic of which I'll never tire. Kayak angling at night presents a set of challenges that can easily be overcome. It also, however, presents an increased risk factor. These risks can also be overcome with planning and common sense.

BUDDY SYSTEM

Whenever possible, go kayak angling at night with a partner, or two. It's a good plan anytime you go fishing but especially helpful under the less-than-optimal conditions found after dark.

LIGHT IT UP

There are so many types of kayak lights out there, it would be impossible to list them all. As of this writing, the US Coast Guard

Many fish species are more active at night, so the fishing doesn't always end at sunset!

requires a flashlight that can be shone at approaching boats. This is not enough. For other small craft, the USCG requires a 360-degree light. I feel this is also the bare minimum for a kayak. Early on in the kayak-fishing world, homemade posts that stuck up well above the angler's head level were the norm. Some kayak anglers also adopted standard stern lights for larger boats that could be run by a miniature 12-volt battery stored below deck. As fish-finders became more prevalent on kayaks, so too did hard-wired lighting. Not everyone wants to wire their kayak for lights and electronics. Some anglers prefer to keep it simple. I appreciate that, but lights are no less important for them. Many battery-powered lights are available to the kayak angler these days, mostly affordable, and complete with clamps for easy installation and removable.

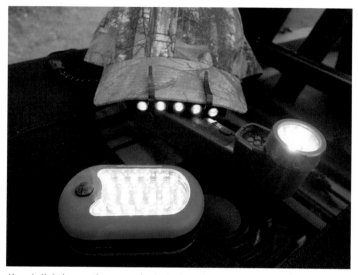

Kayak lighting options can include headlamps, portable LED lights, and standard flashlights.

Navigation aside, you must be visible to other boats.

I feel that kayak anglers should have at least one 360-degree pole light (high enough to be truly visible from 360 degrees), a flashlight, and a mounted light to scan ahead for obstacles or, at the very least, a powerful headlamp. Those sticks, stones, and strainers that are scary enough in daylight can be a real challenge to spot in dark or near-dark conditions. The headlamp can double as a forward-watch light and a handy way to light your kayak interior when changing lures or rigging tackle.

Some kayak anglers have gotten pretty fancy with LED rope lights run along the interior of their kayaks. They are pretty pimpin', as the kids say, and functional. But they're not necessary and don't perform any better than a small mounted light or a headlamp.

A 360-degree light is necessary for nighttime visibility to other watercraft.

Some critics say that the always-on interior lights make it more difficult to see out into the darkness. That makes sense to me.

You may wonder why I mentioned a white stern light on a pole, but not the red-and-green front marker lights. This was done on purpose. On a twelve- or fifteen-foot kayak, front marker lights combined with a stern light may give the impression that you are another boat under power. An oncoming boat may assume that you have the speed and ability to easily get out of their way. You don't want another boater making that assumption. Stick with the 360-degree stern light.

SAFETY

PFDs are the first consideration and have already been discussed at length. Most kayak PFDs come with some reflective strips. Some do not. If you plan on doing any night fishing at all on your kayak, you should consider finding a PFD model that incorporates some type of reflective material. A cell phone in a waterproof case is an absolute must for all kayak fishing but is especially important at night. A whistle should always be in your PFD, as well, to help rescuers locate your position. Don't forget your paddle leash, and your backup paddle. Things are too easy to lose in the dark, and your paddle is one of the only things you truly can't do without! Again, as mentioned earlier in this section, file a flight plan! Let your loved ones or friends know where you're going and when you expect to return. If your plans change, send a text or call to tell them your latest plans. Watch the weather. The wind does not always subside at night. Sometimes it does. But fronts also come through after dark. Be prepared with the knowledge of the evening's forecast.

Watch for boats. Even with your pretty pimpin' light rig, there are bound to be some power boaters out late at night on most bodies of water, especially on weekends, who might not see you. They may be fishermen like you, or partiers who may have been celebrating a bit too much. Watch carefully any boat that seems to be approaching on a dangerous trajectory. Shine your flashlight at the boat and try to attract their attention. If they do not respond by changing course, quickly paddle perpendicularly to their line of travel. Get out of the way!

We're going to talk about landing fish later in the book, but take extra care at night, especially with toothy predators, to handle them carefully. Getting a hook in the hand in the darkness of night is not a pleasant experience. This is where a headlamp, instead of a flashlight, is invaluable. Of course, make sure you always have your side-cutting pliers and first aid kit nearby.

You may want to anchor at night. Some may say it's even more advisable to anchor in the dark to prevent the drifting that you may not notice otherwise. Do so cautiously. Knowing the type of bottom you are fishing is a big help in preventing a snagged anchor, compounded by the confusion of darkness.

Paddling strong current at night is not advisable. In fact, it's really stupid.

Familiarity with the water on which you're night fishing and paddling is imperative, not only for anchoring. The dark of night is not the time to go scouting a new body of water! Reserve your night-fishing trips for local, or at least familiar, waterways.

Be careful out there in the dark. It's a whole different world.

A camera can preserve that once-in-a-lifetime memory, even on darker days.

Anchors and Anchoring

Many of the positive attributes of angling kayaks, such as size, maneuverability, weight, and the ease at which they glide through the water also make them easy targets for abuse by wind, waves, current, or any combination of the three. I don't know any kayak anglers who don't, at least eventually, resort to some type of anchor or anchoring device to stop the boat. Often, breeze and current can be used to the thinking kayak angler's advantage, but there are other times when you simply want to stop and fish. Perhaps there's a fantastic rise of trout on one small pool of a stream. Maybe you've found the panfish hole of all panfish holes and want to park and fill your stringer. Perhaps you would just like to stop and eat your lunch before continuing on. Sooner or later, you will find yourself in the position of wishing you had a way to stay still.

All anchors are cheap and can be readily found in discount outdoor stores. This is one department in which cost is so negligible, you shouldn't have any trouble buying the exact anchor you need for your type of kayak angling.

So, let's look at the options.

GRAPNEL AND FOLDING ANCHORS

I don't like to play favorites when it comes to discussing equipment, but if you don't want to spend a lot of time reading this section on anchoring, just go out and buy yourself a one-and-a-half- or three-pound folding grapnel anchor and be done with it. It's what most kayak anglers use, and for good reason.

The folding anchor has three or four arms or tines that spread out. All the arms or tines can be folded shut and locked against the anchor's stem for storage, or you can use it folded to slow your drift, instead of truly anchoring. It's very small and light, and with its folding capability it takes up almost no valuable space in your kayak. When the (open) anchor hits bottom, it will lay on its side and grip the bottom. It works very well on mud or sand bottoms but may skitter a bit over rocks. A one-and-a-half-pound anchor is the most typical weight you see kayak anglers use; but, if there's wind and heavy surf, or you have an ultralight kayak, a three-pound anchor may be more to your liking. A modified rig I've seen uses a few feet of chain above the one-and-a-half-pound anchor, adding a bit more drag without too much additional weight. By rigging it with carabiners, D-rings, or simple dog snaps, the chain can be removed or added as needed in just a few seconds.

The disadvantage I've found with grapnel anchors (though they are still far and away my favorite) is that they can get hung up on logs and brush piles. And trying to dredge a stuck anchor up and not capsize your kayak can be an exercise in patience.

BRUCE CLAW ANCHORS

The Bruce Claw is another beautifully simple design that uses basic leverage to dig into sandy or silt bottoms. Being less flexible than the grapnel anchor, it is not as useful on rocky bottoms. That said, it's very well suited for use in wind or currents, where the bottom is

Bruce claw (left) and folding-grapnel (right) anchors.

sand, mud, or silt. Typical kayak-angling Bruce Claw anchors will weigh in at about two pounds, which makes them a good selection when trying to keep your kayak load light.

MUSHROOM ANCHORS

If you've ever rented a rowboat or an outboard motorboat, you've probably seen a mushroom anchor. Its shape resembles that of an inverted mushroom. There's no fancy design involved. It drops to the bottom of the lake or river (or ocean) and holds tight by its sheer weight. The size of anchor required to hold a kayak in place under normal conditions is about eight pounds. Now you know why it's not as popular as the grapnel or Bruce Claw anchors. *Mushroom anchors are heavy.* They do have their advantages. They

A basic mushroom-style anchor is another anchoring option.

provide rock-solid anchoring in all bottom conditions (including a rock-strewn bottom). They rarely get stuck, thanks to the rounded design. In high winds or waves, the mushroom anchor is not worth the weight of hauling it around, as its bottom-grabbing properties are virtually nonexistent. The mushroom anchor is a distant third.

ANCHOR LINES AND TROLLEYS

Now that you've selected your (grapnel) anchor, let's talk for a minute about how to secure it to your boat.

Many angling kayaks now come standard with an anchor trolley. An anchor trolley is generally a rope-and-pulley system that runs the length of your kayak on one side (usually the right side, but not always). The anchor line is run through a ring or similar device. The trolley allows the angler to then position the trolley toward the bow or stern. Positioning the trolley (or just a plain anchor rope, for that matter) in the center on one side of the kayak is ill-advised. Gusts of wind, big waves, or a stronger-than-imagined current can pull your kayak and throw you off balance or, worse, swamp the kayak. Kayaks are sleek and streamlined, designed so water runs around the bow and stern with a minimum of resistance. That is why the trolley and/or anchor rope should be positioned near the bow or stern. Also, take care to position the kayak and anchor so the kayak is pulled away by the breeze and current on the side of the trolley and/or anchor rope. Having the anchor pass underneath the kayak in high winds or waves can mean an unintended swim. Take a moment to think about where you're dropping your anchor, where it will end up in relation to the boat, waves, wind, and current, and then think about it again. All it takes is a small bit of common sense

A basic anchor trolley.

to safely anchor your boat. The anchor trolley will allow you to fine-tune your anchor position as well as your fishing position.

Some experts would recommend *never* anchoring your kayak in current. Current, unfortunately, is subjective. Mild-to-moderate current can be safely anchored in, but, as with any anchoring operation, you must pay attention to the current. Swift-current fishing is popular, and those who know how to do it frequently anchor their kayaks in water that I would not. Know your limitations and operate within your experience.

STAKE-OUT POLES

Stake-out poles, also known as 'yak sticks, mud sticks, or stick-anchors (there are other names, too), are simply long, narrow poles used for anchoring in relatively shallow waters, marshes, or flats. There are an increasing number of these on the market, from simple sticks with a lanyard to telescoping lightweight high-tech expensive ones. A DIY stake-out pole can be made from half-inch schedule-40 PVC. Eight feet long will work for most shallow streams and creeks.

A stake-out pole is simply rammed into the bottom next to your kayak. It can be attached to the kayak with a very short length of rope, line, or elastic shock cord. The pole is surprisingly effective at holding the boat in position in shallow water in calm-to-low-wind conditions. It's not effective for every anchoring situation but will prove itself useful enough to become a normal part of your required gear, once you try it. Another advantage of a stake-out pole is the relative quickness with which it can be deployed and subsequently pulled.

You'll see fishermen running their stake-out poles down through a scupper hole. This is not a good idea, despite the apparent convenience. As previously mentioned, scupper holes can be a weak link in the construction of your kayak. Putting undue stress

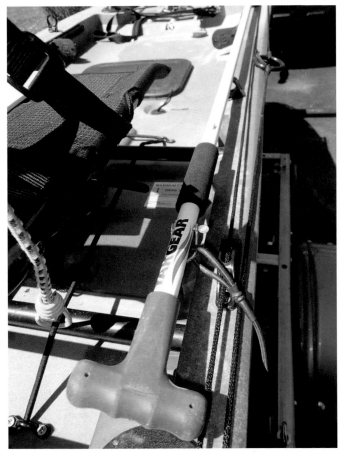

Stake-out pole stored on author's SOT kayak.

on them by having them hold the entire weight of the kayak, as well as the leverage the stake-out pole will apply to the scupper, is taking an unnecessary risk of damaging your kayak. Other kayak experts claim that this practice also reduces stability and can create dangerous situations based on conditions. A grapnel anchor and stake-out pole make a combination that will handle virtually all of your anchoring needs.

TYING OFF AND ANCHOR LINE

Almost any light poly line can work as an anchor rope or stake-out line. I'd advise against using clothesline-type cotton line, as it stretches, doesn't shed water well, and will eventually succumb to mildew and mold. A better option is narrow poly rope. What I like the best is parachute cord. It can be found in big spools, is dirt cheap, and works for a variety of kayak rigging. It's very similar to shock cord, only without the elasticity. Shock cord works fine for stake-out poles, since the distance from kayak to stake-out pole is typically only a few feet.

Many anchor trolleys come with convenient tie-off cleats, and they should be used. As long as the trolley is doing the work of positioning the anchor, it really doesn't matter where the anchor line is tied off—but it should be tied off! After-market cleats added here and there to your kayak will come in handy in many situations for tying down other gear, as well.

Standard knots can be used to attach your anchor to the line, though the addition of clips or carabiners will save time if you need to rig or de-rig in a hurry—or in an emergency.

There's a rule that has been in existence forever regarding anchor line lengths. You won't be surprised to learn that I don't necessarily agree with it. But, if you're interested, it's 7:1. That's seven feet of anchor line for each foot of water in which you are anchoring. 7:1 is not the best ratio for kayaks. Sorry. It's just not. The ideal length of line for your kayak, your anchor, and your situation simply has too many variables for this age-old formula to work in every instance. The truth is, you must let out enough line so that

Stake-out pole and anchor trolley.

your anchor line is not truly vertical in the water. The anchor needs (generally) to lay on its side in order to properly engage the bottom and stop your kayak. Similarly, deploying too much anchor line is also a hindrance. If so much line is deployed that a lengthy amount of time passes before your kayak stops, you're probably past where you wanted to stop. With practice, you can anticipate the longer length's ability to stop the kayak, but it's much easier simply to play it by ear. Your anchor line should angle down and away from your kayak (never under!), enough to allow the anchor to lie on its side. A vertical anchor line is virtually useless. You'll quickly discover what works best for you, and that will vary every time you drop the anchor overboard.

I prefer lighter anchor lines (such as the parachute cord) for safety reasons, as well. If your anchor does get hung up (I've lost two) and is irretrievable, you need a line that can be easily cut, without brandishing a three-foot machete on a twelve-foot kayak. I like minimal gear, but I always have two pairs of side-cutting pliers (one on deck, one in storage below) and a knife. Your anchor line should be of such construction that it's easily cut by your pliers or fishing knife. Most times, a stuck anchor is just a nuisance (I lost both of mine by wedging them in tree roots), but it can also become a dangerous situation in current or wind. Putting all of your might into pulling on your anchor line and risking losing your balance is not worth the price of a ten-dollar anchor. Cut your losses and stay in the boat.

Anchors are cheap.

I'm going to toss this out there (a little anchoring humor), since we've just discussed the best lines to anchor your kayak. I'll admit,

Removing muck from a folding grapnel anchor.

I read this one on the Internet. Instead of a rope, line, or cord, you can use a retractable dog leash, which is available at almost any discount store for a song. It even comes with the clip. You pull the line out and reel it back in. It really is amazing. Keep in mind that the dog leash strapping is a little more difficult to cut through than line, should a snag or an emergency arise. It's probably wise to keep a sharp knife nearby if you adopt this ingenious little trick. Retractable leashes are usually less than twenty-five feet in length, but there are some fifty-footers out there. Line tangling and storage issues disappear. Having fifty feet of anchor line tangled on the deck of an already crowded kayak is a pain and the bane of many kayak anglers who are trying to keep things simplified.

Give it a try!

Folding grapnel anchor and retractable dog leash are the author's anchoring preference.

DRIFT CHUTE

A drift chute or drift sock isn't an anchor, but it fits well with this section. I first used a drift sock while smallmouth bass fishing in a real boat on the big waters of Lake Erie. Even a small drift sock slowed and controlled the drifting bass boat admirably. A drift sock is basically an underwater parachute that attaches to the boat and slows the rate of drift. Its use on a kayak is identical to the way it is employed on a larger boat. It's very useful when fishing large water with a discernible drift pattern. With kayak angling, care should be taken to observe the drift pattern and to deploy the chute in the direction (and side of the boat) *away* from which the natural drift is occurring. As you would with a true anchor, be aware of conditions and waves and be wary of this device that could potentially cause balance issues. Retrieving the drift sock is as easy as pulling it back to the kayak, grabbing the back of the chute, and emptying it out before lifting it aboard.

Whether pulling in (weighing) an anchor or a drift chute, use your arms and keep your head centered over the boat. Again, where the head goes, the body will follow. Keep your head in the boat.

Anchors aweigh!

Part Four

Kayak Fishing

A mix of bait gear and fly gear make for a crowded deck, but an exciting day.

Rigging Your Kayak for Fishing

You've got the basics down: paddling, paddling gear and clothing, and basic safety gear. You've practiced paddling, flipping, self-rescue, and paddling in wind and current, and you have made preparations for varying conditions. I'm guessing that you're ready for something fun. And this part of kayak angling is pretty fun. It's second only in enjoyment—in my opinion—to the fishing itself.

Rigging your kayak for your fishing style and your personality is a lot of fun. Maybe you're a minimalist. A rod holder or two, and you're happy. Or possibly you are a world-class tinkerer and an equipment hound. Either way, or anywhere in between, you'll find that kayak rigging will stimulate your creativity and imagination. In the off-season, you can tinker in your garage, shop, or backyard for hours making small changes for a few dollars here and a few dollars there, until you've created your own ultimate fishing kayak. And then you'll decide to change something else. Therein lies the fun. The ways in which you can modify your fishing 'yak are simply endless. Let's look at some of the basic rigging that you'll commonly see on the water.

Even a well-outfitted SOT fishing kayak can be simple.

THE CRATE

Let's start with the crate because, other than rod holders, the crate seems to be the most uniformly accepted and most expected piece of kayak gear. What started out as bargain-basement storage crates, easily picked up almost anywhere for about five bucks, have since evolved into specialized kayak-specific crates that can run into the hundreds of dollars. Mine is still a five-dollar Home Depot storage crate.

Crates are handy in that you can load them with tackle, sunscreen, food, water, and anything else you might want for a day on the water. They can be easily carried in your car, and then just as easily carried down to your 'yak at the launch area and strapped down. It's an efficient way to store and move a lot of gear.

Many of the crates you'll see in service on angling 'yaks are wearing some kind of rod holder. Many of the more expensive crates come prerigged with them. A very simple way to outfit a

The crate is an integral part of most kayak angling rigs.

cheap crate with rod holders is to buy a cheap single or multirod plastic rod holder and secure it to the crate with zip ties. You can modify the angle of the rod holders to suit your needs, your equipment, and your type of fishing. A crate with a three-rod holder can also be used to carry your rods down to the water. Crates can be very efficient pieces of equipment, and they look pretty cool, too! For ten bucks in total construction supplies, how can you beat that?

Most current angling kayak models (virtually all SOTs) come with a stern platform capable of holding a crate or two. Like all other gear, crates must be lashed down, at the very least with a good bungee cord. Open-top crates are very accessible but also present the risk of dumping your gear in the event that you turtle. Small mesh webbing over the top of the crate can prevent this but also slows access. The specially designed kayak fishing crates often have locking flip-top lids that may prevent loss of gear. I don't

One of the author's crates is a simple, shallow storage bin that provides quick and easy access.

usually put anything I'm afraid of losing in my crate, and I prefer the open-top, old-school version for easy access. Crates should be lashed within an arm's reach behind you.

ROD HOLDERS

The one thing you'll find on nearly every angling kayak is rod holders—usually multiple rod holders. Even very basic models of angling kayaks (such as my SIK) come with some flush-mount rod holders, usually situated behind or adjacent to the seat. Some come preequipped with the Scotty-type rod holders, with which most anglers are familiar. Beyond those two basic types, anglers often add rod holders to their crates and multirod holders at various spots

Very simple three-rod setup in the author's SIK.

on the boat, and anglers who fish in areas with a lot of overhanging trees often outfit their kayak with rod holders that can hold all of their rods horizontally and out of the reach of any troublesome tree branches.

Sometimes I wonder if the people who design angling kayaks have ever tried angling from their kayaks. My recent SOT purchase had everything I was looking for in a new kayak, but it had a rod holder placed in an area in which it made it almost impossible to paddle. And if a rod was in the rod holder? Forget it. The first thing I did was move that rod holder to a better position that didn't interfere with paddling. Beware of rod holders that hold rods vertically too close to your back cast. In my first SIK, I frequently ripped one of the stored rods from the rod holder by snagging it during a back cast. Now, after a few years at this game (and after breaking some stuff), I position all of my stern rod holders over my left shoulder, because 90 percent of my casting finds me casting off the right side of the boat. Another poor design I've found in several models of SOTs is the addition of rod holders so far forward that they can't be reached without crawling or walking the length of the kayak to reach them. If that much effort is involved to get to your rod, you're doing it wrong.

Many anglers, especially those with a brand-new kayak, are hesitant to drill holes in their new purchase. Don't be afraid to install flush-mount holders, but take time and a couple of fishing trips to decide what will work best for you under real fishing and paddling conditions.

Scotty-type holders are a great asset in that they allow varying positions and can be swiveled out of the way or positioned for trolling. However, they also present another piece of gear that can get in the way of your paddle, and it's something else on which you may snag your line. Think carefully about where you position this type of rod holder.

All rod holders should be equipped with rod leashes. Good rods and reels represent a substantial investment, and even if you're using cheap gear, you don't want to lose it in the event of a turtling incident. A rod leash can be a pain to unhook, and the commercially available type seems ridiculously expensive for a piece of shock cord and a clip. I suggest making your own, and using them. Take that fifty-foot spool of shock cord you purchased after reading the earlier section in this book and snip off a few ten-inch pieces. Tie one to the rod holder, and the other to a small clip. Simply clip the cord to itself above your reel, and for less than a buck, you can prevent sacrificing your rods and reels to the water gods.

TACKLE STORAGE

Fishermen like tackle. It's true of tiny dry flies, and true of twelve-inch muskie lures. In a kayak, many anglers prefer to pare back their gear to only one or two of each of their favorite lures, kept in trays and small tackle boxes. Other anglers go whole hog and take one or more large, stocked tackle boxes out with them. There's no right or wrong way when it comes to tackle. In my SIK, I take just a small, basic box (almost like a child's first tackle box) that is jammed full of my favorite lures in several colors. Along with those, I take a tray of basic tackle such as hooks, swivels, and any other hardware that I might need during a day on the water. On my SOT, I usually take more.

Tackle trays (usually purchased more cheaply in discount stores than outdoor stores) are an efficient way to store tackle and hardware. I like a tray for spinnerbaits, a tray for crankbaits and spinners, and a tray for tackle and hardware. When targeting specific species like, say, northern pike, I may make up a tray consisting solely of large, silver stick baits. I recommend buying several of these trays, perhaps twice as many as you plan on using, and

Trays can be sorted and marked by types of tackle, such as this bait fishing tray.

keeping them in storage. You'll find that these minitackle boxes are endlessly adjustable. They're also very easy to store. Four or five of them can fit in your crate and another half-dozen below decks, if you have any storage at all. How many you bring along on your fishing adventure depends on how much weight you want to carry, how easy it is to load your kayak from your vehicle, and what the chances are of needing to switch lures for varying conditions and varying species.

I'm a "go light" kind of guy, but there are days when I bring everything *and* the kitchen sink because I'm unsure of the conditions, typically early in the season. As the fishing season progresses, I might specialize a bit more and take only one or two trays out if I'm targeting specific fish species.

Tackle bags are also a great option, and there are many on the market that fit kayak fishing very well. I have one large bag that has four large trays and many pockets for gear and tools. I consider it the mother ship of my tackle. Sometimes it stays in my truck, and I select just a tray or two to bring along, but sometimes I bring the whole thing, carefully lashing it to the deck, lest I lose an unknown but presumably high dollar figure in lures and tackle.

Some kayak anglers, myself included, have one "go-to" tray, usually stored under the seat or somewhere else within easy reach that contains examples of their favorite and most often-used lures. It's the who's who of tackle, and dipped into often. It's also a handy place into which to drop wet, used lures so they don't need to be sorted or carefully stored away in their proper locations until after the trip is over.

OTHER STORAGE

Dry bags and deck bags are simply waterproof bags that can be stuffed with gear and secured with a bungee cord to the kayak deck. They come in all sizes, from very small cell phone cases to very large duffels capable of holding days' worth of gear and clothing.

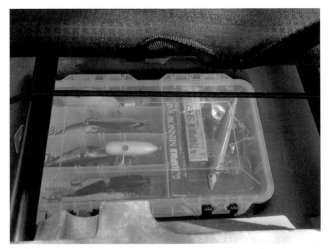

On SOT angling kayaks, frequently used tackle trays can often be stored under the seat.

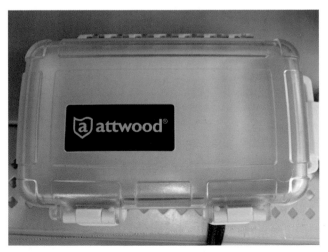

A simple dry box or bag is a must-have for cell phones, wallets, and cameras.

Other options include plastic storage boxes and trays readily available in discount stores, hardware stores, and outdoor outlets. With large angling kayaks, there is almost no limit to what you can bring along, but excessive weight can be an issue both in carrying your kayak and when paddling. Just because you can bring five dry bags and seventeen waterproof boxes doesn't mean you should do it.

TOOLS

The tools you carry depend on the type of fishing you do. I feel the basics any kayak angler should carry are side-cutting pliers, needle-nose pliers, a hook remover, and a knife. The knife and side-cutting pliers can be used to cut anchor line in an emergency (as mentioned previously in the anchoring chapter). The hook remover (of which there are several fantastic designs) is a need based on your type

Handling toothy predators in your kayak should be done with an abundance of caution.

of fishing. The needle-nose pliers can, in a pinch, take the place of both the side-cutting pliers and the fish hook remover. Some redundancy is helpful here, both for safety reasons and for fishing.

Anglers who deal with larger species, whether freshwater pike and muskies, or saltwater anglers who plan on dealing with *really* big fish may wish to employ fish handling devices such as jaw grippers that grasp the fish safely by their jaws for catch and release without risking tooth puncture wounds.

A measuring device (such as the Hawg Trough) is a must if you're a tournament fisherman, and a good idea to keep track of your catches to document your own personal bests. Even a small tape measure will work in a pinch. Adhesive-backed rulers can be mounted to your boat, but the adhesives often don't work as well on plastic kayaks as they do on metal or fiberglass boats.

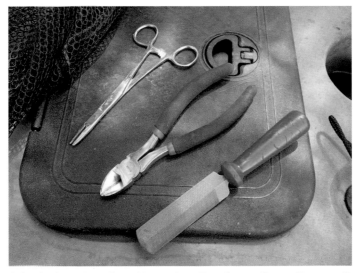

A few basic tools, such as side-cutting pliers, forceps (or needle-nose pliers), and a hook sharpener should come along on every outing.

A "bump board" in the photo makes it hard to lie about how big the fish really was . . . use at your own risk.

NETS

Nets will be mentioned in the fish-handling section coming up, but they just as easily can be listed in the tool section. Nets aren't necessary for every species, such as panfish, but a large, shallow net is a piece of equipment every kayak angler should at the very least keep on board. In the opening section of this book, I detailed an encounter in which a very large rainbow trout took me for a ride. I was rigged for panfish, and the giant trout took me by surprise. Any experienced fisherman will tell you that when you're least expecting it, your small bass lure will be inhaled by a forty-inch pike. I used to pride myself in being able to handle large fish without a net, but in a kayak there are other considerations that make keeping a net handy a very good idea.

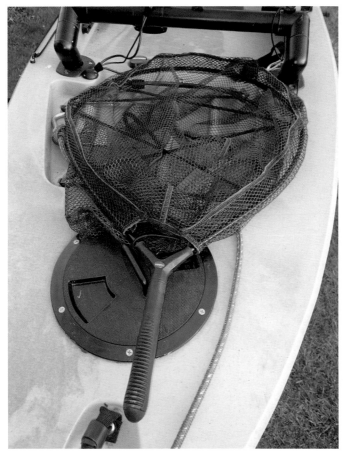

A net is a kayak angling necessity if big fish may be encountered.

Folding nets are a good option if space on your kayak is limited. I like a net with a wide mouth, a short handle, a shallow basket, and made of heavy, nonporous material (such as rubber) that helps prevent those aggravating messes caused by treble hooks and thin netting.

Whether your quarry is bass or fifty-inch muskies, remember to maintain good form to ensure balance.

The shallow net (these are often referred to as catch-and-release nets) makes getting the fish out much easier. An added bonus to a decent net is that the fish can be held underwater until you can prepare your camera for a shot. Keeping fish out of water for an extended period of time while you fumble for your camera or try to adjust your GoPro is needlessly harmful to any fish you plan to release.

Always, when netting, keep your head over the center of the boat and reach out with your arm, scooping the fish headfirst into the net. Pay attention to your balance at all times. Even a five-pound fish can cause havoc with your stability if you are already off-balance.

I like to net-release, as well. I put the fish in the net (if it's been removed at all) and gently lower it back into the water until I'm sure it's revived enough to swim off under its own power. It's a good alternative to leaning out over the kayak (no, no, no!) to revive the fish in a more traditional manner.

CAMERAS AND CAMERA MOUNTS

I've been a fan of photography as long as I've been a fisherman. My fishing and photography pursuits evolved together over the

Author netting a large, aggressive bowfin.

An onboard camera can ensure that your catch-and-release memory is preserved.

decades. Even the coldest, wettest days back in the dark ages of film would find me, at the very least, with a small camera tucked somewhere in a tackle box, fishing vest, or parka. My fishing journey, because of this, has been well documented over the years. Many a friend has suffered, waiting for me to get my camera out to document some moment of a fishing or hunting trip. Not everyone was or is as enthusiastic about fish and fishing photography as I am.

When I first started pursuing kayak fishing, I was pleasantly surprised to see how prevalent cameras were on angling kayaks. I'm not sure why cameras seem so much more common on fishing kayaks than on bass boats or flats boats or even with bank fishermen. What I've surmised is that kayak angling tends to be a solitary sport. Even kayak tournaments consist of several, solitary anglers. In fact, many (or most) kayak tournaments are catch-and-release, and the results are based on photographs of fish on a measuring board. For solo kayak fishermen, it's just a great way to document the day's catch.

With the advances both in digital photography and in waterproof sports/action cameras such as the GoPro and its clones, we're truly in the golden age of self-sports photography. GoPro-type action cameras can shoot high-definition (HD) video and very good photographs, as well. Some can be activated by remote control, or even via smartphone apps. Settings can run the gamut from time-lapse photography to "burst" photography, taking multiple photos as you're landing and releasing a fish. With these advantages, the fish don't need to be out of the water for an extended time to get a good photo before they are released.

The commercially available mounts for action cameras are a fishing photography dream come true. There are gooseneck mounts, tripod mounts, clamp-type mounts, suction-cups, mounts that can be attached to a hat, and long extension poles that allow high- or side-perspective photos and videos. The commercial mounts tend to be fairly expensive, but, fortunately, there's

There are many ways to mount action cameras to a fishing kayak.

One interesting action-cam mount is the "cap-cam."

a wealth of information out there, via the Internet, for plans to make your own inexpensive camera mounts with readily available materials.

In addition to action cameras, there is a whole new world of waterproof cameras out there that can be had relatively inexpensively. In addition to my GoPro-type cameras, I have a point-and-shoot waterproof camera that I also mount on my kayak on one of a couple of different mounts or keep nearby on deck. The camera has several settings, including a self-timer that, once activated, will take a photo every second. When I hook a good fish, I need only push one button. I play the fish, land it, hold it up briefly for the camera, place it in the net, and release it. Never once do I have to pause to get the camera ready—it's been taking photos the entire time. As any photographer will tell you, having dozens of photos

Cameras and electronics are right at home on a modern angling kayak.

to choose from is great insurance that you'll get at least one good photo of your big fish.

With a little care and planning, you can improve the quality of your kayak-angling photos by framing and checking the shots before you even leave home. Sit in your kayak and activate your camera. Check the photos. Did your head get cut off? Is the area in which you'll be holding your fish properly centered in the photo? Is your prized kayak shown in the photos? Once in the water and you have a fish on the line, if it's possible to turn so you are facing the sun before landing the fish, do so. You'll find that the photos are sharper and more vivid if frontlit instead of backlit. Also, take advantage of dramatic sunsets and sunrises to add an artistic dimension to your photos. With a waterproof camera or action camera, think outside the box for interesting photos. I've recently begun taking underwater photos of fish as they are coming in and,

A good alternative to the "grip-and-grin" trophy shot is to photograph and release the fish without removing it from the water. This is a very good option for dangerous and toothy specimens.

sometimes, as they are released. It's a nice alternative (or addition) to the typical "grip-and-grin" fishing photos. If a fish is too large for you to comfortably haul into the boat for a photo, consider a kayak-side shot to document your catch without harming you or the fish.

If you're fishing with a partner, an off-boat perspective makes for good fishing and kayaking photos. Actively take pictures of your paddling and angling partners and encourage them to do the same. Remember to email the photos to one another later in the day so everyone can enjoy them.

Photography and kayak angling are a match made in heaven. Kayaks very often allow a close approach to wildlife in areas where the animals don't often encounter humans in close quarters. Take advantage of those moments and snap a few reference or establishing photos (as photographers call them) of interesting wildlife and landmarks, and you'll find that your kayak fishing photo portfolio will be much more enjoyable to review in the cold months when you can only dream of the coming fishing season.

A fishing partner can assist with that trophy photo.

FISH FINDERS, GPS, AND RELATED ELECTRONICS

Kayak-fishing electronics could fill a chapter all its own. There is so much available to kayak fishermen these days with the smaller, lighter units on the market that to begin to list them all would be an impossibility. Let's cover the basics.

On my current SOT, I've mounted a simple fish finder. It registers depth, water temperature, structure—and fish! It's an amazing, small piece of equipment that takes up a very small footprint on my fishing kayak. It's invaluable for locating drop-offs, schools of bait fish, and changing water temperature, and it is sensitive enough to show my lure and even if any fish are reacting to it. This is essential with fishing tactics such as vertical jigging in deep water, giving you a set of eyes for what is happening far beneath the surface. It suits my fishing style well. It's also has a very bright screen that is clearly visible in bright daylight. This is imperative.

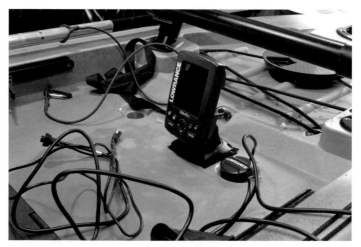

Installation of a fish finder unit can be done in minutes with a little research and ingenuity.

The finished installation.

Other, more complex units incorporate chart plotters, GPS technology, and navigational charts for waters in your area. The GPS and charts can be invaluable when fishing unfamiliar waters and are very effective for night navigation. They can also quickly and easily mark favorite fishing holes to aid in precisely returning to these spots. These units tend to be larger and heavier and require a more solid mounting base than the small units, but I see plenty of kayak anglers using them. It's all in what you require—or want.

I don't find the need for GPS included in the fish-finder package but I do occasionally use my handheld GPS unit for marking hot fishing spots on open water and for keeping track of distance traveled, and so on.

Most kayak anglers these days are using a small 12-volt battery mounted in a waterproof case to power their electronics (and sometimes their lights). Several commercially available boxes are available, but it's very easy to rig a small battery into a small dry box and have excellent results. These small, sealed lead-acid batteries will power your fish finder all day, with power to spare. If the battery is also running lights, or a livewell aerator, the battery life may be reduced, depending on the amount of draw from these devices.

With an SOT kayak, a small 12-volt battery can easily be stored in a hatch.

There's a host of battery chargers available. A serviceable charger with an automatic cut-off to prevent overcharging (which can damage sensitive electronics) will run in the neighborhood of twenty or thirty dollars and is well worth the investment. Avoid uncontrolled "wall wart"-type chargers if possible.

Always ensure that you've read the manufacturer's requirements for hooking your electronic devices to a power supply. Very often an inexpensive inline fuse is recommended for fish-finder installations between the battery and the unit. Don't ignore this step. I'm far from a skilled electrician, but I managed to install an inline fuse in about five minutes. Make certain that your fuse is properly sized for the application, or you'll risk damage to your unit. Wires, if possible, should be run belowdecks on your kayak and out of the way. The fewer obstacles on deck, the better.

Much like fish finders, transducers can be mounted in a variety of ways. I prefer a scupper-hole mount just because it takes up

Battery and charger.

Wire hubs make for a neat transition between storage compartments and the fishing deck.

virtually no space on the kayak deck at all. Other models hang off the side, as you might see in a larger boat. These are fine for most applications but also run the risk of catching on brush or submerged objects in the sometimes very shallow water in which kayak anglers frequently find themselves. DIY transducer mounts abound on the Internet, as well. Do some research, think about your type of fishing and the kind of water in which you most frequently find yourself, and decide what will work best for you.

BAIT BUCKETS

When you first take up kayak angling, you may think the idea of hauling along live bait presents too much of a challenge, at least at

The scupper-hole transducer mount provides a solid, out-of-the-way mounting option for fish-finder transducers.

The scupper-hole transducer mount.

first. There are, however, easy solutions if you're a fan of using live minnows, suckers, shiners, or saltwater baits. A bait bucket in the warm sun on the deck of your kayak may seem like a bad idea, and it can be, but there are other options.

Flow-through buckets have been on the market for a long time, and they can work. I've found that the additional drag on a kayak, however, makes them less than optimal if any amount of paddling is involved. Pulling the bucket out of the water for paddling often causes the high temperature–low oxygen conditions that quickly lead to a bucket full of dead bait.

A standard bait pail can be strapped to the deck of your kayak (preferably in front of you, within easy reach), and a small battery-powered aeration unit can be used to keep your bait fresh all day. I began using this setup a few years ago and found that, even on

Live bait, such as this worm box, is as at home on an angling kayak as any other technique.

the warmest days, almost all of the bait survived a day on the water, especially if fresh water is added every few hours. It's all in the oxygenation, and you'll be amazed at what a difference these small aerators can make. If you're wired for lights and electronics, there are aerators that can also be run from your 12-volt battery. This, of course, will decrease battery life, so you may wish to run the aerator only intermittently.

Finally, the DIY kayak-angling world is alive with bait bucket designs, just as it is with every other aspect of kayak angling. I've seen large coolers converted to livewells and live-bait buckets. I've seen complex aeration systems complete with pumps to exchange the water in the wells for fresh water from the lake or stream. There is no end to the possibilities.

Keep in mind, however, that too much water stored above-deck on your kayak will result in an increasingly high center of gravity, and sloshing water inside your kayak is not your friend when it comes to stability, balance, and additional weight. I'd recommend using the smallest bait bucket you can (mine is about three gallons) and use either a battery-powered or 12-volt aerator. Make sure that it's solidly lashed down, and within easy reach.

Fishing with live bait is a great way to catch many species of fish, both fresh- and saltwater, and there's absolutely no reason that, with a little planning, you can't bait-fish from your kayak.

VHF RADIOS

A good VHF radio isn't an absolute necessity unless you frequent large bodies of water. They can be used to summon help and communicate with other boaters in your area. If you decide to purchase a VHF radio, get the best you can afford and one that is marketed as waterproof. If you need to use it, there's a good chance that you and/or the radio may be in the water.

Bait bucket and battery-powered aerator at home on the author's SOT.

FIRST AID KIT AND PERSONAL CARE ITEMS

A decently stocked first aid kit is a good idea for a backpack or your car, but when it comes to kayak angling, a first aid kit becomes even more important. Not only dealing with elements of the outdoors, kayak anglers find themselves contending with the hazards associated with knives, spiny fins, hooks, rope burns—and teeth! A well-stocked kit should consist of a couple of rolls of gauze, adhesive tape, antiseptic wipes, burn cream, bandages, and a pair of scissors. With these items, you can cover most puncture wounds, which are the most common fishing injury.

I won't get into a first aid lesson here, but suffice it to say that the water in which our fish-friends swim is anything but sterile. Quickly flushing a wound with bottled water and then treating with antiseptic wipes and antibacterial cream is a very good idea. Any serious wounds, of course, should be attended to by a medical professional as soon as possible.

First aid classes are readily available, and I highly suggest taking them. At the very least, read a good book on the subject. There are several small manuals that can easily be kept in one of your dry storage areas and that may prove invaluable in the event of a more serious injury.

In addition to a first aid kit, depending on the season, keep your kayak well stocked with bug spray and sunscreen. Skin cancer is a real danger for all fishermen, and a small bottle of sunscreen takes up practically no space. Also, with the virulent spread of tick- and mosquito-borne diseases in the last few years (and just so the bugs won't make you crazy!), always bring along a bottle of bug spray, even during the coldest months.

A first aid kit is a necessity for all outdoor adventures, especially those involving sharp hooks . . . and teeth!

A couple of bottles of water are a necessity to keep yourself in good paddling shape and to fend off dehydration. I also like to tuck a granola bar or two into one of my dry bags for those times when you didn't *think* you'd need to eat while out fishing but your stomach is loudly proclaiming otherwise.

LIGHTS

Please refer to the paddling at night chapter (see page 203) for detailed lighting suggestions for low-light kayak angling. Just as a refresher, remember to have a stern-mounted white pole light that is high enough to be seen for 360 degrees. Avoid green and red bow lights, as these could give the impression to other boaters that your kayak is a larger, more agile boat. Keep a flashlight handy to warn off approaching boats. Utilize a headlamp or dedicated deck-mounted light to illuminate obstacles ahead of the boat.

RACKS AND TRACKS

A quick ten minutes of research will reveal a dizzying array of mounting tracks and homemade racks or bars on which your cameras, fish finders, lights, rod holders, and other gear can be mounted. As of this writing, universal track mounts are becoming increasingly popular among serious kayak anglers.

I recently constructed a DIY project of PVC for a front-mounted bar, on which I can mount my cameras and a rod holder, as well as a rear rack that can accommodate my stern light as well as a three-rod rod holder. These bars were both installed into the factory flush-mount rod holders. It's a bastardization of an idea I got when looking at what a friend of mine was using. My idea was to get as much gear within easy reach without overcrowding the deck of the kayak. It seemed to make sense to go *up*. So far, so good.

Electronics and camera mounted on author's homebrewed "rack" system.

The author's do-it-yourself rod rack on his SOT angling kayak.

As mentioned multiple times, the ways in which you can customize your kayak are limited only by your imagination.

COOLERS

Coolers are a cool addition to any fishing kayak. Not only can they keep your food and drinks safe, but a large cooler can be used to hold your day's catch or to keep your live bait, such as night crawlers and worms, alive for the duration of your kayak angling outing. With the array of coolers on the market today, there's something to fit your need.

Soft-side coolers are popular, and the newer models are not only more efficient at staying cool but also much easier to strap securely to your kayak deck than hard-sided coolers, and they are easier to store out of sight when not needed.

A small, soft-side cooler is ideal for kayak angling.

Hard-sided coolers, especially midsized models, are popular with kayak fishermen due to their cold retention properties as well as their durability. Resist the urge to overload them, however, because with each pound of ice and food you add, you're raising the overall weight of the boat and, as described in the bait-bucket section (see page 248), you may alter the center of gravity enough to affect paddling performance and stability.

Some intrepid anglers have gone so far as to replace their seat with a cooler to further decrease the clutter on their already burgeoning kayak decks. The coolers are often used as a standing platform, particularly by flats-fishermen, dramatically raising their height and aiding in sight fishing. And, I must assume, dramatically increasing the chance they're going swimming.

That's a bit too adventurous for me.

Specially designed cooler bags that are shaped and designed to ride on the bow or stern of the kayak are also increasing in popularity. These are frequently used to hold fish that aren't to be released (dinner, for example), and they also work well for your daily food and drink needs. Their low profile also helps aid in wind-resistance, something at which a large, rectangular hard-sided cooler is definitely not adept.

Kayak Fishing!

can't teach you to fish (even if it feeds you for the rest of your life). If you're reading this book, you're already a fisherman and you have decided to take it to a different level with kayak angling. With all of your gear purchased (and secured, and wear your PFD!), you've practiced paddling, rolling, and recovery and you've notified your friends or family where you're headed. This is the moment we've all been waiting for. It's time to take that fishing kayak fishing.

Perhaps you spend your days on the saltwater flats looking for redfish. Maybe you're haunting inland ponds bobbing minnows for perch and crappie, or hunting elusive monster pike in a backwater creek. Maybe there's nothing more fun to you than landing a good bass on a spinnerbait or a trout on a dry fly. Whatever type of fishing it is that floats your kayak, I'm making the assumption that you're already pretty good at it. With so many species and specialties (even within the bass-fishing or fly-fishing fraternities, for example), it would be an exhaustive study to examine how all of them translate to kayak angling. If you've ever watched YouTube videos of goliath grouper coming in on a kayak angler's line, you know that there's simply no limit to applying your type of fishing to kayak fishing.

If you can catch it, you can catch it in a kayak!

I won't presume to tell you how best to enjoy your favorite type (or types) of angling in a kayak. However, there are some tips I can share that are universal among all types of kayak angling.

TACKLE ORGANIZATION

Even the largest kayaks with virtually unlimited storage capabilities still offer limited space in which to practice your sport. Neatly organizing your tackle into several small boxes or trays that are readily accessible, either in your crate or a nearby storage hatch, is a necessity.

I'm primarily a freshwater fisherman, and my go-to pike and bass tackle (my two favorite warmwater species) are organized into three major categories. One tray is heavily crammed with crank baits, both in silver and perch-color. These are what I use to catch pike and bass day in and day out, and I have a healthy selection of thin and fat, jointed, and jerk bait styles. A second box contains spinnerbaits. I'm a spinnerbait addict. There aren't nine different colors. There are three. And there are a couple of each color. Simple. In the spinnerbait box, I also have some spoons for open water trout and pike fishing, and some small spinners that might find their way on to my ultralight rod if things are slow. In a third box, I have tackle. There are hooks of a few different sizes, swivels, snaps, steel leaders, weights of all descriptions. It's my tackle box. These three trays of my main fishing arsenal are complemented by a small tackle box that probably looks like the first tackle box you or your kid had as a child. It has a single plastic tray on top. The tray contains side-cutting pliers (two pairs), needle-nose pliers, and a hemostat (I love a hemostat for hook removal). In the main part of the silly little tackle box, you'll find a few spools of line and a bunch of other oddball stuff that I may or may not need during the course of the day fishing. All four of these boxes are within reach of my kayak seat at all times. If I'm doing some specialty fishing like lake-trout or stream-run salmonids, or soft-jigging for small-mouth bass, I may fill an entirely different tray with the specialized equipment, lures, and tackle that I need. That's all part of the fun. In my truck, I keep a monster-sized tackle bag with a full complement of every type of lure, bait, and tackle I use. I used to take the whole bag out with me on my kayak angling outings but quickly realized that it's overkill in terms of weight, footprint, and gear. You can simplify your tackle trays for kayak angling and still be well prepared for whatever conditions and lure needs that might come along. Leave the "mother ship" tackle bag at home, or in your vehicle, if you can. If you're like me, you'll feel a little naked at first but will soon realize that things can be much easier.

Large "mother ship" tackle bags can be left in a vehicle, or strapped to the kayak for extended days on the water.

I like to mark the tackle trays with a simple "SB" (spinners/spinnerbaits) or "CB" (crankbaits) or "Tackle" on the edge or edges that will be most visible, depending on how you have them stored. I've used this trick for years, long before I took up kayak fishing, and it saves time pulling out tray after tray, hoping you get the right one.

Another aspect of tackle organization I try to employ regards what to do with "used" lures. At some point during the day, despite the fact you've brought along a half-dozen rods rigged with a little of everything, you're going to probably want or need to change lures to suit the conditions. Another trick I've used for many years is to keep a small container, whether an open tray, a recycled yogurt container, or plastic coffee can, and drop my unwanted lures, spinners, or plastics into it. The container is a handy way to keep loose gear off of your deck, for neatness' sake. It also eliminates the hassle of putting the lure back in its proper place while you're trying to fish. Doing that during preparation for your next outing is half the fun. You can take your time, rinse the lures, remove bits of unwanted lines and knots—all on your own time later. Better to not cut into fishing time if you can help it. It also provides a place to dry the lures before they go back in your tackle boxes or trays, where wet gear tends to cause premature corrosion.

TACKLE SELECTION

As stated at the outset of this chapter, I'm not going to try to teach you how to fish. Over the years, I've developed a few favorite lures and tactics that work well with kayak angling, and they have one thing in common—simplicity. There's that word again. You can apply this concept to your angling whether your pursuit involves sailfish or sunfish. My current go-to rig in a kayak for my type of angling is a spinnerbait. Forget the fact that it works well for bass, pickerel, pike, bowfin, and walleye in my home waters. It does, but it's also very simple. There's one hook. If you break it off, it's easy to tie another one on. You can tune it to run properly by simply bending wire with your fingers, and its big hook and steep angle offer easy removal from a fish's mouth. To me, it is simply the lure that has it all. Look for gear like that for your kayak angling selection. Avoid complexity if you can.

I also like a drop-shot rig. It's basically the same hook-and-weight system you used to fish bait when you were ten years old. Fancy name for a hook and a sinker, but it's a very versatile rig. On recent trips, I've fished it with live bait, plastic baits, and worms and caught a *lot* of big fish. Again, like my spinnerbait love-fest, it's just a simple rig. If you break it off, it takes less than a minute to get a new rig up and running (if those tackle trays are within easy reach!).

Many kayak anglers are avid spoon fishermen, as well. Why? They're simple, for all of the reasons listed above.

BAIT FISHING

In the rigging chapter of this book (see page 223), we talked a lot about bait buckets for your kayak, so we won't delve too deeply here. Bait fishing is a time-tested way to catch every species of fish that can be caught. Most of us learned to fish by drowning worms under red-and-white bobbers.

For the kayak angler, bait offers yet another simple solution. Whether it's night crawlers, crabs, or shrimp in your cooler or bait-fish in an aerated bucket or livewell, bait is still one of the best methods going to catch fish, and it translates very well to kayak angling. It has all the hallmarks of simplicity to which kayak angling is so well suited. You procure bait, either by catching or purchasing (cast-netting for bait from your kayak is a lot of fun, if you have the time); you need some hooks, a weight, and maybe a float; and you're in business. It doesn't get much simpler than fishing with bait. When the bait is doing the work, rather than you, you'll find plenty of time for paddling, casting, adjusting your position, or working on your tan. It's one of the most relaxing methods of fishing that can also turn into one of the most explosive and productive methods, if the conditions are right. And, when it comes to bait, the conditions are almost always right!

TROLLING

Can you troll open water in your kayak? You sure can. With side-mounted rod holders, your kayak can be an efficient trolling machine. With the addition of side-planers or Dipsy Diver-type rigs, a fairly complex trolling arrangement can be undertaken. Even slow angling kayaks are capable of speeds that are conducive to taking species typically targeted by larger trolling boats. With the kayak more susceptible to winds and waves, an eye must be kept toward weather and conditions to troll most efficiently, of course.

If your kayak is outfitted with chart-plotters (or a handheld GPS) and a fish finder, this can help in targeting the areas most likely to hold fish. Listening to local fishing reports and targeting the depths at which the fish have been recently active with your trolling rig can make your outings much more productive.

Finally, trolling is a great way to get experience paddling your kayak!

FLY FISHING

I could write an entire chapter (or maybe a whole book) on fly fishing from a kayak. One of my first kayak-angling outings found me fly fishing for brook trout in a small mountain lake. I'd read up quite a bit about kayak angling, and most of what I read said that fly fishing was very difficult—*especially* in sit-inside kayaks. At the time, all I owned was my first SIK angling kayak. Several articles said that if you didn't have an SOT, you might as well not even try to fly fish. Further, if you couldn't stand on your SOT, then you should probably just stay home.

Fly fishing lends itself surprisingly well to kayak angling. As always, good form is everything.

I'm glad I hadn't listened. Fly fishing in an SIK or an SOT is easy. Like other fishing techniques, it might require a bit of adjustment in technique, but it's far from impossible. Actually, I find it rather enjoyable.

Like kayak angling, fly fishing, for all of its mysteries, is all about simplicity. All of my fly-fishing gear for an entire weekend trip fits in a small bag and a rod case. How could this sport *not* align perfectly with the simplicity inherent in kayak angling? The two, in fact, go together perfectly.

If you're a stand-up SOT angler, you just go out and fly fish. That simple. If, however, you are in an SIK or not comfortable standing in your SOT, a slight adjustment in casting is required. Good fly-fishing form requires a good, high backcast. Good kayak fly fishing requires that the cast be a bit higher to prevent contact with the water's surface on the backcast, due to the lower angle from which you're casting. It took me all of five minutes to develop a fly-casting technique that worked fine in my SIK.

Author in his SOT with a good fly-rod brown trout.

I sometimes ridicule rod selection criteria for kayak angling. I will concede that, with kayak fly fishing, a slightly longer rod is helpful in keeping your fly line off the water until the cast is complete. Most fly anglers have many rods anyway. If you have a seven- and eight-foot rod in your collection, perhaps choose the eight, for example. If you don't, spend five minutes as I did developing your technique and then just get out there and fish.

Fly fishing from a kayak is an adventure in and of itself. Try it!

WADING

Many anglers enjoy wading for trout, bass, or panfish. Wading pairs well with kayak angling. In my area, for example, there are many Lake Ontario tributaries that are very deep and wide at the mouth but narrow and shallow in the upper reaches. Some of these upper reaches are not easily accessed by foot and are often prime spawning spots for trout and salmon. It's not uncommon for a day of fishing to start with some deeper casting for trout and pike, then to paddle up into the shallower water to jump out and wade the shallow water in search of the spawning giants. An SOT kayak makes transitioning from water to kayak and back very easy, though I've certainly done it plenty of times from my SIK, as well.

WEED ANCHORING IN THE SLOP

Many anglers love to fish the slop—dense weeds and lily pads—for bass and other species. Traditional anchors tend to become a messy affair when dropped into weeds. Often your two-pound anchor comes up with ten additional pounds of muck. A stakeout pole is a distinct advantage in this situation (if the water is shallow enough to reach the bottom), but there's another anchoring technique that we've not discussed yet: weed anchoring.

This simple technique involves simply running the bow of your kayak into some lily pads or other thick vegetation in close proximity to where you're going to cast. The kayak will hold surprisingly steady—even in the wind—because of the added friction of the weeds. There's no anchor to fight with, and when you're ready to move on, you need only paddle back out of the weeds—or farther in, if you so desire.

RODS AND REELS

I recently read a very serious article on rod selection for kayak angling. I'm sorry, but come on! Do you need a slightly shorter, longer, heavier, lighter, faster, slower rod for kayak angling than if

Weed anchoring is a quick and dirty alternative to anchor and anchor line.

you were to fish from a bigger boat? Why would you? Some would argue that the light nature of an angling kayak demands a heavier rod for hook sets. I am here to tell you that you can set a hook just fine with whatever rod you were using before you bought your first angling kayak. I see now a couple of manufacturers are offering "kayak angling" rod-and-reel combos. It made me laugh, but I'm sure someone will buy them. Seated kayak fishermen have a bit lower of an angle for casting and hook setting, to be sure, but it's more an adjustment in technique than it should be another three hundred bucks out of your wallet to get the latest . . . kayak rod. Sorry, I'm still laughing. Whatever your target species requires in a rod is what you should be using. And, even then, any experienced fisherman will tell you about the twelve-pound trout or twenty-pound pike that took them by surprise while they were fishing with an ultralight rig and four-pound test—and how they landed it. Don't overthink your rod selection. Use a good rod that works well for you.

Casting from an SOT kayak.

There is no reel that will make you a better kayak angler. Well, I guess I should say that I'm a fan of good reels, for all applications. When I was younger, I didn't think too much about things like a smooth drag or line capacity. I also lost a lot of fish because I didn't think about those things. Great Lakes steelhead and salmon are notorious for ripping off line and knowing just when to surge when you've accidentally pinned your line to the rod. A good drag on spinning, baitcasting, and fly-fishing reels is a must for me. For small fish and smaller species, it isn't ever much of an issue. But with larger species, a good drag can save the day by tiring the fish without breaking it off, if set properly.

Testing your reels' drag systems the night before each of your angling outings should become part of your ritual. All you need to do is pull on the line with the reel closed (or locked) and make sure the drag gives before the line breaks. It really is that simple. If it doesn't, adjust until it does. You'll frequently see good fishermen adjusting the drag while fighting fish. I do this, as well. There's a point at which you may want to put more pressure on the fish, and a tighter drag is the way to go, provided the fish has been worn down a bit. Don't overdo it, but practice this technique. Too *little* drag can also make for a bad day, especially with species like trout and pike that make last-minute runs once they're within sight of the boat.

If I had any suggestion to make regarding reels used in kayak angling, it would be to set the drag ever so slightly *lighter* than you might while bank fishing or fishing from a larger boat. Once you've hooked into a good fish in your kayak, it can pull the boat about pretty easily. A lighter drag will allow the fish to get some distance before having a large effect on your position. Of course, if you're fishing with an anchor, this probably won't be an issue, though you may get pulled in circles and the anchor line can sometimes get in the way. Many experienced kayak anglers will take a moment to drop their anchor when they realize they have hooked a large fish. I don't tend to do this and would rather play the fish even if it means kayak position getting manhandled a bit. If, of course, the fish is headed toward current, rocks, or submerged timber, it may be a good idea to drop your anchor or stakeout pole and make a stand before you find yourself in an aggravating situation.

FIGHTING FISH

Fighting fish in a kayak is only slightly different from fighting fish under any other circumstance. What needs to be kept in mind while fighting a fish in the kayak is only that you must maintain good kayak *paddling* form during that time. I've heard many stories of kayak anglers being "pulled under" by medium-sized game fish. How is it, then, that those open-ocean kayak anglers manage to stay dry while landing hundred-pound tarpon?

I'll tell you: good form.

Do I need to say this again? *Where the head goes, the body will follow.* If you keep your head centered over the kayak and your feet planted firmly and evenly spaced, and you stay in your seat (unless standing), you'll be fine. You don't need to lean over the side of your kayak. With most 'yaks, the water is within arm's reach and most fish can be lifted into the boat from the seated position. I hooked a forty-five-inch northern in current last year and brought him up to the side of my SIK. When I realized that I'd left my camera's memory card at home (yes, I'm still kicking myself), I released the brute without hauling him in. If I'd had the card, however, his picture would be right here. It's not hard to land big fish in a small boat. It does, however, take some planning.

Use a net. As mentioned in the rigging chapter (see page 234), I always have a large catch-and-release net. I don't use it for bass, unless they are big and I want to hold them in the water long enough to set up a photo. The net serves as the perfect buffer zone to keep fish healthy while you prepare that hero shot. As with hand-landing, though, resist the urge to lean over the boat when netting. Guide the fish headfirst into the net with line pressure,

Good kayak paddling form is necessary when casting. Where the head goes, the body will follow. Keep your head centered!

and keep your head centered over the boat. It takes a bit of practice to resist that urge to lean over and look at your hard-won fish, but it's essential to staying dry that you do just that.

Good form and balance is also necessary when netting big fish.

I'm not going to preach here, but also consider releasing that fish. I love a good perch dinner and ate a couple of smallmouth bass for shore-lunch not too long ago, but treat your fishery and the individual fish with the respect they are due. There are a lot of fishermen out there competing for those fish. As for individual respect, try to get the fish back in the water as fast as possible. With a little practice, I've gotten pretty quick with catching, netting, photographing, and releasing the fish. If a fish appears to be not responding to being revived underwater, give it a few extra seconds of "hold time." Often that's all it takes to make the difference between a live fish and a floater. We owe the animals we pursue, whether in hunting or fishing, to be treated humanely. And, please, don't ever *throw* your fish back. I've seen this too many times, especially in tournaments. Just don't do it. A little respect for your catch is easy.

All fish that will be released should be handled quickly and efficiently to reduce stress on the animal before it's returned to the water.

KEEPING FISH

So you've heard my speech on catch-and-release. Let's talk about catch-and-eat-dinner. While I heartily endorse catch-photograph-release of game species, especially trophy-sized fish, I also like to eat fresh fish. There are plenty of species out there who are suffering no shortages, such as the various panfish species and others. And sometimes, author-be-damned, you're just going to want to eat that trout dinner you've craved all winter. So, how do you do it?

Some inventive anglers have put livewells on their kayaks! You don't have to go that far, but you can if you want to. A cooler strapped to the stern with some ice is a decent alternative for keeping fish fresh. Many kayak anglers employ the age-old chain-stringer for fish they intend to eat. It can be lifted from the water for extended paddling, but can also be left in the water without causing a great amount of resistance. A new wave of deck bags (also

Spincasting for trout, early season.

called deck coolers) is designed with kayak aerodynamics in mind. They can be filled with ice and easily accessed from the kayak seat, usually via a zipper, and are an interesting alternative to stringers or hard-sided coolers. They often come with integrated tie-downs, making them a perfect addition for a kayak angler who likes to keep his catch.

Keeping a mess of panfish for dinner is easily accomplished with a stringer and/or a small cooler.

Final Thoughts on Kayak Fishing

I like kayak fishing. I like it a lot, in fact. By now you've probably realized that. My love of the sport is the driving reason that, earlier in this book, I wrote about my annoyance with certain trends in kayak angling leaning toward snobbery. There's a reason for that: I want kayak angling to be accessible to everyone, not just the guys who can afford a thirteen-hundred-dollar kayak. I want everyone with five hundred bucks to spare to think to themselves, "Damn, that really sounds like fun. I want to try it."

Please, try it.

Once you're sucked in—and you will be, I promise—invite your spouse, your friends, and your extended family to join you. Kayak angling is a rapidly growing sport, and that is mostly because it's accessible to all cross-sections of society, despite income, it's a great way to catch fish, and it is a lot of fun. Fun can't be put high enough on the list of reasons to kayak angle. Landing a big fish or a whole bunch of small fish in a small plastic boat is a thrill. How

Kayak angling offers unlimited challenges and unlimited fun!

many things do you have in life that you can call a thrill? Besides the fishing aspect, there's the ability to quietly spend time nature, with only the soft *plop plop* of your paddle as you move forward, on

Big water kayak angling at sunset.

to the next fishing hole. Take in the scenery, and enjoy the quiet of an early morning encounter with a loon, or the dazzling brilliance of an evening sunset. Most of all, *relax.* It's only fishing.

Index